MORE ABOUT THE

USA

A CULTURAL READER

MILADA BROUKAL
JANET MILHOMME

Longman

More About the USA: A Cultural Reader

Addison-Wesley Longman, 10 Bank Street, White Plains, NY 10606

Photo credits: Page 3, The Gamma Liaison Network/Photo by Erik Hill © Anchorage Daily News; page 9, Photo by Francesco Scavullo ® Harpo/King World 1994–1995, All Rights Reserved; page 15, ™ & © Lucasfilm (LFL) 1981, All Rights Reserved. Courtesy of Lucasfilm Ltd.; page 21, All rights reserved, The Metropolitan Museum of Art, The Alfred Stieglitz Collection, 1949; page 27, UPI/Bettmann; page 33, National Baseball Library & Archive, Cooperstown, N.Y.; page 47, Courtesy of the Library of Congress Geography and Map Division; page 53, Death Valley National Monument; page 59, Photo by Jimmy Walker; page 65, The Bettmann Archive; page 79, The Bettmann Archive; page 99, NASA; page 105, March of Dimes Birth Defects Foundation; page 117, © National Air and Space Museum, Smithsonian Institution, Photo No. A 26767 B-2; page 125, Image of Elvis used by permission, the Estate of Elvis Presley.

Editorial director: Joanne Dresner
Acquisitions editor: Allen Ascher
Development editors: Kathleen Sands Boehmer, Françoise Leffler
Senior production editor: Carolyn Viola-John
Production editor: Janice L. Baillie
Text design adaption: Curt Belshe
Cover design: Sue Moore
Cover credits: Top row, left to right: The Gamma Liaison Network/Photo by Erik Hill © Anchorage Daily News; National Baseball Library & Archive, Cooperstown, N.Y.; The Bettmann Archive. Center row, left to right: © National Air and Space Museum, Smithsonian Institution, Photo No. A 26767 B-2; NASA; Death Valley National Monument. Bottom row, left to right: Image of Elvis used by permission, the Estate of Elvis Presley; Courtesy of the Library of Congress, Geography and Map Division; March of Dimes Birth Defects Foundation.
Text art: Laura Hartman Maestro
Photo research: Brian Huss

Library of Congress Cataloging-in-Publication Data

Broukal, Milada.
    More about the USA : a cultural reader / Milada Broukal. Janet Milhomme.
      p. cm.
    ISBN 0-201-87679-5
    1. Readers—United States. 2. English language—Textbooks for foreign speakers. 3. United States—Civilization—Problems, exercises, etc. I. Milhomme, Janet. II. Title.
PE1127.H5B695   1995
428.6'4—dc20
                                      95-24398
                                      CIP

ISBN: 0-201-87679-5

2 3 4 5 6 7 8 9 10-CRS-989796

CONTENTS

INTRODUCTION

More About the USA is an intermediate reading skills text for students of English as a Second Language. A host of facts about the USA presented within the themes of people, places, living things, great moments, and culture, not only provide students with information about the USA, but also stimulate cross-cultural exchange. The vocabulary and structures used in the text have been carefully controlled at an intermediate level, while every effort has been made to keep the language natural.

Each unit contains:
- Prereading questions and introductory visuals
- A reading passage (520–820 words)
- Topic-related vocabulary work
- Skimming for main ideas
- Scanning for details
- Order of events
- Making inferences and drawing conclusions
- Discussion questions
- A writing assignment
- Research assignments

The prereading questions are linked to the visual on the first page of each unit. They focus the students on the topic by introducing names, encouraging speculation about content, involving the students' own experience when possible, and presenting vocabulary as the need arises.

The reading of each passage should, ideally, first be done individually by skimming for a general feel for content. The teacher may wish to deal with some vocabulary at this point. A second, more detailed individual reading could be done while working through the vocabulary exercise. Further reading(s) could be done aloud by the teacher or with the class.

The VOCABULARY exercise encourages students to work out meaning through context and then check with a dictionary. If the meaning is clear through context, there is no need to check with a dictionary. However, occasionally there are words that are too difficult to be guessed through context, and a dictionary will be needed. This will prepare students to deal with vocabulary in an authentic text. As suggested previously, this section can be done during the reading phase or afterwards or both.

There are four kinds of COMPREHENSION exercises: *Skimming for Main Ideas* helps students confirm the basic content of certain paragraphs. This can be done either individually, in pairs, in small groups, or as a whole class. *Scanning for Details* concentrates on the scanning skills necessary to derive maximum value from reading. *Order of Events* concentrates on developing a sense of organization of the reading and develops the skill of spatial organization. *Making Inferences and Drawing Conclusions* develops the skill of inferring meaning from what is not directly stated in the passage by reading "between the lines."

DISCUSSION gives the students the opportunity to bring their own knowledge and imagination to the topics and related areas. They may wish to discuss all of the questions in their small groups or to select one on which to report back to the class.

WRITING consists of a composition assignment. *Composition* develops the students' writing skills that are closely linked with reading by expressing their own ideas about a composition topic related to the reading.

RESEARCH continues and expands the theme of the passage by giving students an opportunity to do their own research. Students can work in pairs or groups and give reports on their findings.

Additional Assignment Suggestions:

A Summary: This written exercise (this exercise can also be done orally) focuses attention on expressing the main ideas of the passage in the students' own words. Students write a one-paragraph summary of the reading, focusing on the key points in the reading and making sure that all the main ideas are discussed in the summary. Students must not copy from the reading.

Restatement: This exercise provides the opportunity to practice the newly-learned vocabulary in a clearly constructed paragraph. A particular paragraph is chosen in the reading. Students read the paragraph several times and then restate the content in their own words in writing (can also be done orally).

PEOPLE

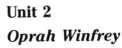

SUSAN BUTCHER ON THE IDITAROD TRAIL

Look at the picture. Do you know what this sport is? Do you think this sport is dangerous?

What other snow sports do you know?

1   An hour into the race, Susan Butcher and her **sled dog team** speeded down a hill, **skidded off** the trail, and crashed into a fallen tree. With a hurt shoulder, Susan **untangled** her sled and team of Alaskan husky dogs and continued the **grueling** race across the frozen Alaskan wilderness. It was the fourth year she had run this race, known as the Iditarod, and she wanted very much to win it.

2   The history of the Iditarod goes back to 1925 when a doctor in Nome, Alaska, was **desperately** in need of medicine to stop the spread of a deadly disease called diphtheria. Only a hospital in Anchorage, 700 miles away, had the supplies he needed. But it was January, too dangerous to send a boat across the frozen Bering Sea and too stormy for his tiny airplane. The only hope was to use sled dog teams following an old native **trail** through the mountains and tundra. The medicine was passed from one man and his sled team to another along the trail. It was named Iditarod after one of the towns

SUSAN BUTCHER ON THE IDITAROD TRAIL   3

it passed through. Storms of wind and snow, and temperatures as cold as 60 degrees below zero, did not stop them, and the medicine was delivered in record time. Most of the Iditarod Trail Sled Dog Race follows the route of the famous medicine run. It is over 1,000 miles long, and is considered the toughest race in the world. In 1978 Susan Butcher entered it for the first time.

3   Susan Butcher was born in 1954 in Cambridge, Massachusetts, and had a love of animals and the outdoors from the time she was a child. She was athletic and loved to sail. She often imagined herself sailing around the world by herself. Little did she know what she would really end up doing. In her teens Susan was given a Siberian husky dog and became very interested in the history of huskies as sled dogs. At the age of 17 she moved to Colorado where she began to train and run dogs for a racing **kennel**. After reading about the Iditarod race in a magazine, Susan moved to Alaska. She worked at several jobs to earn enough money to buy herself a sled and team of huskies. Susan achieved her dream of being in the Iditarod after years of hard work and **vigorous** training.

4   In her first race in 1978 she finished 19th and became the first woman to finish in the top 20. The following year she finished ninth, and the third year in fifth place. In her fourth race in 1982 she came in second. The next year she again finished in the top 20. In 1984 she was leading her team across a frozen waterway when suddenly the ice began to shake and fall apart. Susan and her team fell into the **frigid** water. Her lead dog managed to get to shore and pulled Susan and the other dogs out of danger. Susan's clothes were soaked and already starting to freeze. Nevertheless she kept going, running for a while to dry her clothes, then riding the sled so her lungs wouldn't freeze from her heavy breathing. Remarkably, she pulled into Nome in second place.

5   In 1985 many people thought Susan would win. However, it was not to be. On the trail, she met a starving moose, which is a very large hoofed animal of the deer family, that attacked her dogs, killing two and injuring eleven. Susan had to leave the race. That year, it was another woman, Libby Riddles of Teller, Alaska, who became the first woman to win the Iditarod. In 1986 Susan joined the race again. This time her lead dogs fell off a shelf of ice. Susan managed to rescue them and kept going through blinding snow storms. Sometimes she was so tired she began to imagine things, such as a forest where there was none. More than once she lost the snow-covered trail. But others did too, and Susan won the race. She won again in 1987. In 1988 she became the first ever to win three Iditarod races in a row. Unbelievably, Susan became a winner for the fourth time in 1990. Her strength, **stamina,** and dedication had made her the most famous dog sled racer in the world.

VOCABULARY

Complete each definition with one of the following words or phrases. Guess your answers, then check with a dictionary.

sled dog team	skidded off	grueling	trail
untangled	desperately	vigorous	
frigid	kennel	stamina	

1. A person with _____ has a strong body or mind to fight tiredness and keep on going.

2. Extremely cold is _____ .

3. A place where dogs are kept is a _____ .

4. A group of dogs working together to pull a small vehicle for sliding along snow is a

   _____ .

5. If a vehicle _____ the road, it would have slipped sideways out of control.

6. Exercise that demands a lot of force and energy is _____ .

7. A path across rough or wild country is a _____ .

8. Something that is very hard and exhausting is _____ .

9. When something is _____ , the twisted parts are made free.

10. To suffer from extreme need of something is to need it _____ .

COMPREHENSION

A. Skimming for Main Ideas

Circle the letter of the best answer.

1. Paragraph 2 is mainly about
   a. the history behind the Iditarod race.
   b. the difficulty of transportation in Alaska.
   c. the suffering of the people in Nome, Alaska.

2. The main topic of Paragraph 3 is
   a. Susan Butcher's move to Colorado.
   b. Susan Butcher's life up to the time of her first Iditarod race.
   c. Susan Butcher's love of dogs and her work with them in Colorado.

3. The main topic of Paragraph 4 is
   a. Susan Butcher's historical win in 1978.
   b. Susan Butcher's accident on the trail in 1984.
   c. Susan Butcher's top 20 finishes in spite of all odds.

4. The last paragraph is mainly about
   a. Susan Butcher's courage and determination leading to her success.
   b. Susan Butcher meeting disaster and being forced to leave the 1985 race.
   c. Libby Riddles becoming the first woman to win the Iditarod.

B. Scanning for Details

Scan the paragraphs for details. It is not necessary to read the whole passage again. Some of the following sentences have incorrect facts. Cross out the incorrect fact and write the correct answer above it.

1. The Iditarod Sled Dog Race is over 3,000 miles long.

2. The history of the Iditarod began in 1940 when a doctor in Anchorage, Alaska, was desperately in need of medicine.

3. At 17 Susan Butcher moved to Colorado and went to college to become a veterinarian.

4. In her first Iditarod race, Susan Butcher became the first woman to finish in the top 20.

5. A plane couldn't be used to get the necessary medicine for measles because they couldn't find a pilot.

6. In 1985 Susan had to leave the race after a starving moose attacked her dogs.

7. In 1988 Susan Butcher became the first person ever to win three Iditarod races in a row.

8. Susan Butcher moved to Alaska after someone offered her a job.

9. In 1984, even after falling into freezing cold water, Susan Butcher continued the race and came in second.

10. The Iditarod Trail is named after the doctor who sent for the medicine.

C. Order of Events

Number the sentences to show the correct order.

———— Susan Butcher moved to Colorado and began training dogs.

———— Susan Butcher moved to Alaska.

———— Medicine was carried along the difficult and dangerous Iditarod trail.

———— People were in danger of getting the deadly diphtheria disease.

———— Susan Butcher entered her first Iditarod race.

———— Susan Butcher became the first person to win three Iditarod races in a row.

———— Susan Butcher read about the Iditarod race.

D. Making Inferences and Drawing Conclusions

The answers to these questions are not directly stated in the passage. Circle the letter of the best answer.

1. From the passage, it can be concluded that
   a. Susan Butcher could probably have won the Iditarod when she was still in her teens.
   b. it takes years of training to develop the strength and ability to win an Iditarod race.
   c. the Iditarod race is the kind of athletic event that almost anyone can enter and have a chance to win.

2. It can be inferred from the passage that
   a. it was because of the courage and determination of the men and their sled teams that the people of Nome were saved.
   b. other forms of transportation would have been more successful than the sled teams in bringing medicine to Nome.
   c. it was too late to save the people of Nome by the time the medicine arrived from Anchorage.

3. The passage implies that
   a. Susan Butcher achieved success as a result of courage, hard work, and determination.
   b. the 1984 Iditarod was an easy race for Susan Butcher to win.
   c. Susan Butcher was well known even before she began participating in the Iditarod races.

DISCUSSION

Discuss the answers to these questions with your classmates.

1. Why do some people risk their lives at a sport?

2. What other sports involve animals? Do you think it's cruel for animals to be used in sports?

3. Do you think men and women should compete against each other in a sport?

4. What other winter sports heroes do you know? What are they famous for?

WRITING

Composition: Choose a popular or special sport that is played in your country. Describe when and how the game is played, and why it is popular.

RESEARCH

Look up the following dangerous sports. Explain what dangers are involved in each.

1. Bungee jumping
2. Skydiving
3. Rock climbing
4. Extreme skiing
5. Cliff diving
6. Hang gliding

OPRAH WINFREY

Do you like to watch television talk shows?

What is your favorite talk show?

What subjects do they discuss on talk shows?

1   Oprah Winfrey is one of the most exciting, highest paid, and best-loved celebrities in America. She is also the country's top television talk show host. Oprah Winfrey is a very fine actress and a successful producer. She is a living example of what talent, hard work, and determination can do.

2   Oprah Winfrey has come a long way from her poor childhood home in a small Mississippi town. She was an unwanted child whose parents never married. She was brought up on her grandmother's farm. The possibility that she would become rich and famous was not very good.

3   Oprah's mother left her child in her mother's care, so she could go to work in Milwaukee, Wisconsin. It was a strict and difficult life for Oprah. But it also led the way for her future. She was a highly intelligent child. By the age of three, she had learned to read and write. She also made her first public appearance at that age. She gave a talk in church, which impressed everyone. "That child is gifted," people said.

4   Oprah's intelligence was **resented** by other children her age. They called her unkind names and pushed her away. Oprah felt very isolated and

unwanted. It made her feel worse that she didn't live with her mother and father. She felt that no one loved her. This made her angry, resentful, and **rebellious**. These feelings brought her much trouble as she was growing up. She often behaved badly, causing her grandmother to punish her. By the time Oprah was seven, she was too much for her grandmother to discipline. Then Oprah went to live with her mother, Vernita, in Milwaukee.

5   Vernita worked very hard at her job as a housekeeper. It was hard for her to work and take care of her bright, troublesome child. Oprah was a burden, and she knew it. They lived in poverty in a small apartment in the city. Oprah took out all her angry feelings on her mother. She was a difficult child. When Oprah was eight, Vernita sent her to live with her father and stepmother in Nashville, Tennessee. But she was moved again a few months later when Vernita married a man with two children. Vernita wanted Oprah with her and her new family.

6   Unfortunately Oprah felt she didn't belong with them. She believed she wasn't loved by anyone. Her anger and **frustration** grew stronger. She **struck back** by misbehaving and running away from home. Her parents found her impossible to discipline. When she was 14 they tried to send her to a special center for troubled girls. But there was no room for her. So Vernita sent Oprah back to live with her father. Vernon Winfrey was by then a successful businessman and family man. He took one look at his daughter and knew she needed guidance, love, and discipline. He gave her all three. It was a turning point in Oprah's life. Vernon was strict about his daughter's education. He gave her homework in addition to her schoolwork. She was allowed to watch only one hour of television a day. She became an A student and a popular girl in her class.

7   Oprah watched Barbara Walters, a famous journalist and interviewer, and decided that was what she wanted to be. When she was still in high school, she got a part-time job reading news on the radio. In her senior year she won a beauty contest and a four-year scholarship to Tennessee State University. While still in college she was offered a job as a news broadcaster at a local television station. She was the first female and the first African-American newscaster in Nashville. She was **promoted** to anchor, the most important position on the news team, while still a senior.

8   After Oprah graduated she got a job with a Baltimore news station. But she soon realized that broadcasting news wasn't enough for her. She had to let her personality shine through. She wanted to show emotion when she told a story, not just report it. Meanwhile the station managers were feeling the same way. They couldn't stop her from **commenting** on the news she read! They removed her from the anchor spot and wondered what to do with her. Finally they put her on an early morning talk show called *People Are Talking*. No one knew what to expect.

9   The show was a great success. In a very short time, the managers and Oprah all knew what she was born to do. She was funny, **witty**, charming, warm, and **compassionate**. She was everything a **talk show host** should be. She was so successful that she got a show with a bigger station in Chicago. It was called *A.M. Chicago*. Within one month the show's **ratings** were the best in years. Twice she left the show to make movies, *The Color Purple* and

Native Son. In 1985 the show was changed to *The Oprah Winfrey Show*. It was broadcast nationally and soon became the most popular talk show on television. By the age of 35, Oprah Winfrey was one of the most famous celebrities in America.

VOCABULARY

What is the meaning of the underlined words? Circle the letter of the correct answer. Use a dictionary to check your answers.

1. Other children her age <u>resented</u> her intelligence.

    a. were impressed by

    b. felt angry about

    c. made fun of

2. Oprah became angry and <u>rebellious</u>.

    a. disobedient

    b. bitter

    c. impatient

3. Her anger and <u>frustration</u> grew stronger.

    a. strong determination

    b. intense dislike

    c. annoyed disappointment

4. She <u>struck back</u> by misbehaving.

    a. went on

    b. responded

    c. held on

5. She was <u>promoted</u> to the position of anchor on the news team.

    a. given a temporary position

    b. transferred

    c. advanced in position

6. They couldn't stop Oprah from <u>commenting</u> on the news.

    a. giving her own opinion

    b. changing the facts

    c. making jokes

7. Oprah was funny, <u>witty</u>, and charming on the show.

    a. tender and loving

    b. clever and humorous

    c. curious about things

8. She was also warm and <u>compassionate</u>.

    a. sympathetic to others

    b. polite to people

    c. amusing

9. Oprah was a great <u>talk show host</u>.

    a. person who introduces famous celebrities on television

    b. person who has his or her own show on television

    c. person who introduces and talks to other people on TV

10. The show had the best <u>ratings</u>.

    a. selection of celebrities

    b. rank given according to popularity

    c. variety of subjects to discuss

COMPREHENSION

A. Skimming for Main Ideas

Read these paragraphs quickly to find the main ideas. Circle the letter of the best answer.

1. Paragraph 3 is mainly about
   a. Oprah's life with her mother.
   b. Oprah's childhood with her grandmother.
   c. Oprah's school years.

2. The main topic of Paragraph 5 is that
   a. Oprah became a burden to her mother.
   b. Oprah wanted to live with her father.
   c. Oprah's parents worked hard.

3. Paragraph 7 is mainly about how
   a. Oprah won a beauty contest.
   b. Oprah admired a famous journalist.
   c. Oprah started her career in broadcasting.

4. The main topic of the last paragraph is that
   a. Oprah became a great success and celebrity.
   b. Oprah starred in two movies.
   c. *A.M. Chicago* got the best ratings after Oprah joined the show.

B. Scanning for Details

Find the details to complete these sentences as quickly as possible. It is not necessary to read the whole passage again.

1. Oprah's mother left Oprah with her grandmother, so she could go to work in

   _____.

2. By the age of three, Oprah had learned _____.

3. At the age of _____, Oprah left her grandmother's house and went to live with her mother.

4. Oprah misbehaved so much that when she was 14, her parents tried to send her to

   _____.

5. Today, Oprah is one of the country's most popular

   _____.

6. Oprah's life began to change for the better when she went to live with

   _____.

7. Oprah had roles in two movies, _____ and

   _____.

8. In her senior year in high school, Oprah won a scholarship to

_____ .

9. Before Oprah was given a morning talk show, she had a job as a

_____ .

10. Oprah's morning talk show was a great success because she was funny,

_____ , _____ , _____ ,

and compassionate.

C. Order of Events

Number the sentences to show the correct order.

_____ Station managers at a Baltimore news station put Oprah on an early morning talk show.

_____ Oprah misbehaved and ran away from home.

_____ Oprah lived on her grandmother's farm in Mississippi.

_____ Oprah's father gave her the guidance and discipline she needed.

_____ Oprah got a part-time job reading news on the radio.

_____ Oprah went to live with her mother in Milwaukee.

_____ Oprah became the first female and the first African-American newscaster in Nashville.

D. Making Inferences and Drawing Conclusions

The answers to these questions are not directly stated in the passage. Circle the letter of the best answer.

1. From the passage, it can be concluded that

    a. Oprah's childhood was easy compared to her adult life.

    b. Oprah's father was an important influence in her life.

    c. Oprah's poor background kept her from achieving her potential.

2. It can be inferred from the passage that

    a. Oprah's personality made her a better newscaster than a talk show host.

    b. the traits that made Oprah successful appeared at a young age.

    c. Oprah was unable to overcome her problem childhood after she grew up.

3. The passage implies that

    a. if Oprah had been a better newscaster, she might have been more successful.

    b. Oprah's personality and intelligence were the two main factors that brought her success.

    c. Oprah's bad behavior as a child was a result of being spoiled by her mother and grandmother.

DISCUSSION

Discuss the answers to these questions with your classmates.

1. The subjects discussed on many talk shows are very personal. Do you think these subjects should be discussed on television? Why or why not?

2. Why do you think talk shows are so popular?

3. If you were a talk show host, whom would you like to interview? Why?

4. What factors do you think are important for a person to become rich and famous?

WRITING

Composition: Give two reasons for or against having talk shows on television.

RESEARCH

Find out what the following African-Americans are famous for.

1. Rosa Parks

2. Martin Luther King, Jr.

3. Whoopie Goldberg

4. Ray Charles

5. Wilma Rudolph

6. Barbara Jordan

7. Bill Cosby

8. Colin Powell

LUCAS AND SPIELBERG AT THE MOVIES

Unit 3

Do you like to go to the movies?

What are your favorite movies?

Who are your favorite movie stars?

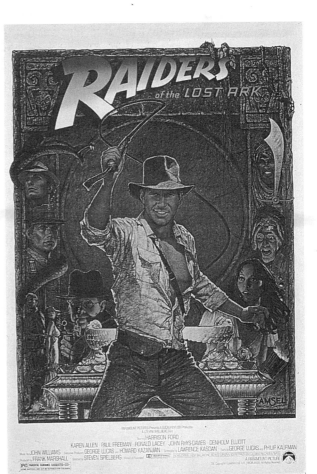

1 The great white shark silently approaches the **unsuspecting** swimmer. The audience of *Jaws* screams in fear of the moment when those huge teeth will snap shut and pull the victim under the waves. On the screen a few years later, the **forces** of good and evil fight against each other in a faraway **galaxy** in *Star Wars*. Space people come to earth in *Close Encounters of the Third Kind*. Later, Indiana Jones has wild adventures in *Raiders of the Lost Ark*. From outer space to the ocean's depths to imaginary treasure hunts, the movies of George Lucas and Steven Spielberg have entertained audiences for over 20 years. Moreover, these movies changed the direction of American film forever.

2 Lucas and Spielberg both achieved fame as the brightest young **talents** in Hollywood in the late 1970s and early 1980s. Two of their greatest films, *Star Wars* and *Close Encounters of the Third Kind,* appeared in the same year, 1977. Both men were named for an Academy Award. The two science fiction

films used **special effects** that had never been seen before. Special computerized cameras were invented and miniature models of spaceships and cities were designed. The effects on-screen kept audiences breathless. When Lucas and Spielberg worked together on the action-adventure films *Raiders of the Lost Ark* and its **sequel** *Indiana Jones and the Temple of Doom*, they once again **captured the imaginations** of the audience and made them feel as if they were a part of the action. This is what made their films so successful.

3   In a way, you can say that Steven Spielberg was a born filmmaker. He was born and grew up in Cincinnati, Ohio, and had all the interests of American boys his age. But he also had an extraordinary desire to make films. Steven was not a good student. He spent more time watching and making movies with his father's camera than he did studying. His grades were so poor that he couldn't get into film school, so he went to study English at a state college in Los Angeles. Once again, he spent all his time going to movies. He **sneaked** onto movie sets in Hollywood to watch directors at work, and made his own small films. One film, called *Amblin'*, was noticed by film executives and gave Steven his big **break**. He was signed to a seven-year contract to direct television movies.

4   George Lucas, on the other hand, never gave a thought to making movies. Born in Modesto, California, he dreamed of being a race car driver. But three days before his high school graduation, he was in an accident that nearly killed him. He had to give up his car racing dreams. He went to Modesto Junior College, where he became interested in film work. A friend encouraged him and helped him get admitted to the film department of the University of Southern California. There he made a short science fiction film that won him first prize in a film festival. It got him started in the film business when it was later developed into a full-length film, *THX 1138*.

5   They were two very different boys with very different dreams. Lucas and Spielberg are friends today and are still among the brightest and most talented directors in Hollywood. Both have made great contributions to the art of filmmaking. Already **legends** in their time, they are sure to continue their fine work for many years to come.

VOCABULARY

Complete each definition with one of the following words or phrases. Guess your answers, then check with a dictionary.

unsuspecting	forces	talents	sequel
galaxy	special effects	break	
legend	sneaked	captured the imagination	

1. If a person is not aware that something is going to happen, he or she is

   _____ .

2. Any large group of stars in the universe is a _____ .

3. People who have a special natural ability or skill in a particular field or area are

   _____ .

4. Something that follows something else as a continuation of it is a

   _____ .

5. When someone gives you a _____ , you get a chance or an

   opportunity.

6. Visual or sound effects that are put into a motion picture are _____ .

7. A person who is very famous in a particular area becomes a _____ .

8. Powers that may produce change are _____ .

9. _____ is when a person went somewhere quietly and secretly.

10. If a movie held your interest as if it were real, it _____ .

COMPREHENSION

A. Skimming for Main Ideas

Circle the letter of the best answer.

1. Paragraph 1 is mainly about
   a. how the movies of Lucas and Spielberg entertained audiences.
   b. how outer space adventures make popular movies with people.
   c. the importance of good and evil in movies.

2. The main topic of Paragraph 2 is
   a. how Lucas and Spielberg achieved success.
   b. the two science fiction films that Lucas and Spielberg created.
   c. why special effects are important in movies.

3. The main topic of Paragraph 3 is that
   a. Steven Spielberg was a poor student.
   b. Steven Spielberg was a born filmmaker.
   c. Steven Spielberg began to direct television movies.

4. Paragraph 4 is mainly about how
   a. Lucas' dream was to become a race car driver.
   b. Lucas began his career with a science fiction film.
   c. Lucas became a filmmaker by chance.

B. Scanning for Details

Find the details as quickly as possible and circle the letter of the correct answer. It is not necessary to read the whole passage again.

1. When George Lucas was a boy, he dreamed of becoming
   a. a race car driver.
   b. a movie producer.
   c. a scientist.

2. Steven Spielberg was born and grew up in
   a. Hollywood, California.
   b. Cincinnati, Ohio.
   c. Modesto, California.

3. George Lucas first became interested in film work
   a. in Hollywood.
   b. at Modesto Junior College.
   c. at the University of Southern California.

4. The forces of good and evil fight against each other in
   a. *Jaws.*
   b. *Raiders of the Lost Ark.*
   c. *Star Wars.*

5. *Star Wars* and *Close Encounters of the Third Kind* were both what kind of film?

   a. science fiction

   b. comedy

   c. action-adventure

6. One of the things that made the films of Lucas and Spielberg so successful was

   a. good actors.

   b. special effects.

   c. interesting movie locations.

7. Steven Spielberg wasn't a good student because he spent most of his time

   a. racing cars.

   b. playing sports.

   c. making movies.

8. Lucas and Spielberg both achieved fame in the

   a. late '70s.

   b. late '80s.

   c. early '90s.

9. One of the ways in which Lucas and Spielberg created special effects was by using

   a. real sharks.

   b. pictures of outer space.

   c. computerized cameras.

10. Before Spielberg became famous for his movies, he worked as

   a. a television director.

   b. an English professor.

   c. a model maker.

C. Order of Events

Number the sentences to show the correct order.

_____ Lucas and Spielberg worked together on *Indiana Jones and the Temple of Doom*.

_____ George Lucas was admitted to the University of Southern California.

_____ *Raiders of the Lost Ark* was produced.

_____ The movie *Star Wars* was made.

_____ George Lucas made the film *THX 1138*.

_____ Lucas and Spielberg were named for Academy Awards.

D. Making Inferences and Drawing Conclusions

The answers to these questions are not directly stated in the passage. Circle the letter of the best answer.

1. From the passage, it can be concluded that

   a. Lucas and Spielberg both showed promise as filmmakers in their youth.

   b. Spielberg became a filmmaker because he did too poorly at school to do anything else.

   c. Lucas and Spielberg have had a major influence on the films we see today.

2. It can be inferred from the passage that

    a. Lucas and Spielberg followed traditional ways of filmmaking in their most popular films.

    b. the types of films Lucas and Spielberg made in the 1980s would not be popular today.

    c. Lucas and Spielberg are both highly creative individuals.

3. The passage implies that

    a. science fiction films are more popular than action-adventure films.

    b. audiences like to feel as if they are part of the action.

    c. audiences don't like to be frightened by movies.

DISCUSSION

Discuss the answers to these questions with your classmates.

1. Do you think there is too much violence in films today?

2. Do you prefer to go out to the movies or to watch a video at home? Why?

3. Do you like movies with special effects? Do you think they're better than the old movies that didn't have the use of such technology? Give reasons for your answers.

4. Which type of movie do you like best: western, science fiction, action-adventure, or romance? Discuss your reasons.

WRITING

Composition: What is your favorite movie? Tell the story and give reasons why you like it.

RESEARCH

The following are names of famous film directors and producers. Give the names of two movies they are famous for.

1. Alfred Hitchcock   **3.** Francis Ford Coppola   **5.** Spike Lee

2. David Lean   **4.** Clint Eastwood   **6.** Michael Douglas

GEORGIA O'KEEFFE— ART LEGEND

What kind of paintings do you like?

Who are your favorite painters?

Do you know of any famous women painters?

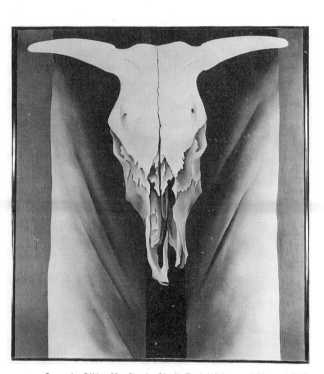

Georgia O'Keeffe, Cow's Skull: Red, White and Blue, *1949*.

1   In the 1930s Georgia O'Keeffe was voted one of the twelve outstanding living women, along with Eleanor Roosevelt and Helen Keller. By the 1960s she was considered one of the greatest living artists. In the 1980s she was still living and still painting. By then she had become an American legend.

2   Georgia O'Keeffe was born in 1887 in a Wisconsin farmhouse, the second of seven children. She was independent, **willful**, and she often **misbehaved**. She went places she was told not to go, like the **barnyard**. She did things she was told not to do, like eat dirt. She was sent to her room with only bread and milk for supper. But she only said, "I like bread and milk." Later in life, Georgia's life on the farm would influence her painting, such as when she painted parts of cornplants and flowers.

3   From the time she was nine, Georgia and her sisters were driven in a horse-drawn carriage to their art teacher's home. It was thought important in those days for young ladies to study art so they could decorate their homes. However, Georgia took her lessons more seriously than that. She had bigger plans for herself.

4   The O'Keeffes eventually moved off the farm to Williamsburg, Virginia. Georgia, with her love of the outdoors, was not happy there. She loved to swim and sail and fish, and unlike other Southern girls, did not wear hats or gloves to block the sun. She was very unlike her classmates, who wore **frilly** dresses and spoke with Southern accents. Georgia was a simple farm girl who dressed as plainly as she spoke. No matter how much her classmates tried to change her, she refused.

5   Within only a few weeks at her new school, Georgia was receiving special attention from Elizabeth May Willis, the headmistress and art instructor. She recognized O'Keeffe's talent and eventually became one of the many people who helped O'Keeffe during her life. In other areas, though, O'Keeffe was very badly behaved. She fought with the girls and **disrupted** their studies. She taught others to play card games. She ate dirt, as she had as a child, and had **temper tantrums**. Once, she burned some of her drawings, saying that one day she would be famous and didn't want those pictures around when it happened.

6   O'Keeffe's belief that she could become a famous artist was rare among women of her time. It was accepted that women art students would become teachers. Actually, O'Keeffe did take a job as an art instructor after her studies in New York. First she was an instructor at a school in Amarillo, Texas, and then at West Texas State Normal College. While in Texas she began painting landscapes. For the first time she created art with a unique style, unlike anything she had been taught in school.

7   In 1918 she moved to New York, where her work was already starting to be noticed. In just a few years she was **praised** as the greatest woman artist of her time, the first woman artist to **excel** in America at a time when most artists were men. She painted in bright colors and a modern style, and every day became more famous. But she was still different. She wore men's clothes and long black dresses. She didn't talk much. When she did, she was often angry. It was the only way she knew how to express herself, other than through her art.

8   In 1924 she married Alfred Stieglitz, a famous photographer, 24 years older than O'Keeffe. The two great artists were very much in love but found life together very difficult. They often separated for long periods of time. He stayed in New York and she went to New Mexico, where she found **inspiration** for her work. After Stieglitz died in 1946, O'Keeffe moved to New Mexico permanently.

9   She lived in an **adobe** house in a tiny village called Abiquiu, at the end of 20 miles of dirt road. It had spectacular views of the New Mexico landscape, of the mountains and valleys, of sunrises and sunsets. It was here that Georgia O'Keeffe lived an isolated life for the next 30 years and produced her greatest works of art. She became the best-known American woman artist of this century, more famous than even she had ever imagined.

VOCABULARY

What is the meaning of the underlined words? Circle the letter of the correct answer. Use a dictionary to check your answers.

1. Georgia O'Keeffe was an independent and willful child.
   a. a person who is thoughtful of others
   b. a person who does what he or she likes in spite of other people
   c. a person who plans things in advance

2. She often misbehaved.
   a. did wrong or bad things
   b. said funny things
   c. got confused

3. She went to places she was told not to go, like the barnyard.
   a. a yard near the railroad
   b. a building where tools are kept
   c. a yard on a farm with a fence around it

4. O'Keeffe did not wear frilly dresses or speak with a Southern accent.
   a. with a lot of embroidery
   b. with a lot of gathered decorative edging
   c. colorful

5. Georgia O'Keeffe fought with the girls and disrupted their studies.
   a. interfered with
   b. controlled
   c. helped with

6. Georgia O'Keeffe had temper tantrums.
   a. loss of consciousness
   b. fits of anger
   c. periods of depression

7. O'Keeffe was praised as the greatest woman artist of her time.
   a. licensed
   b. recommended
   c. admired

8. She was the first woman artist to excel in America at a time when most artists were men.
   a. surpass
   b. be equal
   c. be inferior

9. She went to New Mexico, where she found inspiration for her work.
   a. objects
   b. scenery
   c. ideas

10. O'Keeffe lived in an adobe house in a village in New Mexico.
    a. made of earth and straw
    b. made of stone
    c. made of wood

COMPREHENSION

A. Skimming for Main Ideas

Circle the letter of the best answer.

1. Paragraph 1 is mainly about
   a. other outstanding women of Georgia O'Keeffe's time.
   b. Georgia O'Keeffe as an outstanding woman.
   c. Georgia O'Keeffe as a great artist of the 1960s.

2. The main topic of Paragraph 7 is
   a. O'Keeffe's move to New York.
   b. O'Keeffe's personality and progress as an artist.
   c. O'Keeffe's choice of fashions and manner of speaking.

3. The main topic of Paragraph 8 is
   a. Alfred Stieglitz's fame as a photographer.
   b. O'Keeffe's move to New Mexico.
   c. O'Keeffe's marriage to Stieglitz.

4. The last paragraph is mainly about
   a. O'Keeffe's isolated life in New Mexico.
   b. the landscape around the village of Abiquiu.
   c. the kind of works produced by O'Keeffe during the last 30 years of her life.

B. Scanning for Details

Scan the paragraphs for details. It is not necessary to read the whole passage again. Circle T if the statement is true. Circle F if the statement is false.

1. When Georgia O'Keeffe was growing up, there were many famous women artists.	T	F
2. After moving to Texas, Georgia O'Keeffe developed her own unique style of art.	T	F
3. When Georgia was growing up, she was a quiet, well-behaved child.	T	F
4. Georgia O'Keeffe was born in 1887 in Wisconsin.	T	F
5. Georgia always got along well with her classmates.	T	F
6. O'Keeffe liked to use dark colors and a traditional style of painting.	T	F
7. Georgia's early years on a farm influenced her painting when she became an adult.	T	F

8. By the 1960s Georgia O'Keeffe was considered one of the greatest living artists.   **T   F**

9. O'Keeffe's husband, Alfred Stieglitz, was an important politician.   **T   F**

10. From the time she was a young girl, Georgia O'Keeffe believed she would be famous.   **T   F**

C. Order of Events

Number the sentences to show the correct order.

_____ Georgia O'Keeffe moved to New York.

_____ Georgia and her sisters were driven to their art lessons in a horse-drawn carriage.

_____ Georgia O'Keeffe married Alfred Stieglitz.

_____ O'Keeffe moved permanently to New Mexico.

_____ The O'Keeffe family moved to Williamsburg, Virginia.

_____ Georgia O'Keeffe was voted one of the twelve outstanding living women.

_____ O'Keeffe taught art at West Texas State Normal College.

D. Making Inferences and Drawing Conclusions

The answers to these questions are not directly stated in the passage. Circle the letter of the best answer.

1. From the passage, it can be concluded that

    a. Georgia O'Keeffe had a unique personality all of her life.

    b. O'Keeffe led a very traditional way of life.

    c. O'Keeffe's talent didn't show until she went to New York to study painting.

2. It can be inferred from the passage that

    a. Georgia O'Keeffe was brought up in a time when women were not trained for careers.

    b. O'Keeffe was famous for only a brief period in her life.

    c. Stieglitz and O'Keeffe had a happy and contented life together.

3. The passage implies that

    a. what influenced Georgia O'Keeffe's art style the most was the training she received at school.

    b. O'Keeffe was a friendly woman who liked to be around people.

    c. O'Keeffe expressed her thoughts and emotions through her art.

DISCUSSION

Discuss the answers to these questions with your classmates.

1. Many famous artists have been known to be eccentric and live strange lives. Can you think of any? Do you think this is true of most artists?

2. Abstract art can sometimes consist of a spot of paint on a canvas. Some people think this is not true art. What do you think?

3. There are some people who believe painting can be learned. Others believe it is a gift you are born with. What is your opinion?

4. What were some of Georgia O'Keeffe's personality traits? How do you think they helped her to become a famous artist?

WRITING

Composition: There are many styles of art, such as impressionistic, classical, and abstract. What kind of art style do you like? Give reasons and examples.

RESEARCH

For each of the following modern art movements, find two artists who are famous for that style.

1. Impressionism
2. Cubism
3. Pop art
4. Surrealism
5. Fauvism

THE BIRDMAN OF ALCATRAZ

Do you know about any famous criminals?

Do you know about any famous prisons?

Why might a person be given the nickname "Birdman"?

Robert Stroud (center) with guards.

1   The story of Robert Stroud has been written many different ways. Some say he was a troubled boy from a broken home who accidentally killed someone. Others say he was a cold, **vicious** man, a murderer who should have been **executed**. Others fall somewhere in the middle. All of them agree on one thing, though. Robert Stroud is one of the most famous American criminals of all time.

2   Robert Stroud was 19 when he killed a man in a dispute over a dance-hall girl in Juneau, Alaska. He was **sentenced** to 12 years at McNeil Island Prison in Washington state. Prison life was hard. After two years there, Stroud **stabbed** a fellow prisoner who had told the authorities Stroud was stealing food from the kitchen. Six months were added to his sentence. In 1912 he was transferred to Leavenworth Prison in Kansas.

3   Stroud had received only a third-grade education. Some people thought he was stupid, including his cell mate who was taking some correspondence

courses. Stroud decided he would like to do the same. Within three years he had received diplomas from Kansas State University in engineering, music, mathematics, and theology. Stroud was now prepared for his release in the near future.

4   In March 1916, shortly before he was to be freed, Stroud killed one of the guards. He had been very angry over not being able to see his brother, who had come all the way from Alaska to visit him. He was tried, found guilty, and sentenced to hang. Stroud's mother would not accept this. She petitioned President Woodrow Wilson and his wife. She impressed them with descriptions of her son's studies. Just eight days before he was to hang, Stroud's sentence was changed to life in **solitary confinement**.

5   One day Stroud found two baby birds in the exercise yard at Leavenworth. He raised them with the help of bird books. From that point on, his interest in **ornithology** became a passion. He bought some canaries, did experiments in canary diseases, and studied and wrote about his findings. After a while, prison officials tore down the wall between Stroud's cell and another empty cell to make more room for Stroud's canaries. He obtained laboratory equipment and studied chemistry, veterinary medicine, and bacteriology.

6   By 1931 Stroud was an expert on the care and raising of canaries. He corresponded with other bird lovers all over the world. He wrote some articles that were **smuggled out** of prison and published. In 1942 he published a book called *Stroud's Digest of the Diseases of Birds*. It was considered the best work in the field. Meanwhile, Stroud's work was making him very well known. Too well known. People began to ask for Stroud's release. This angered some prison officials.

7   In 1942 Stroud was transferred to Alcatraz. He was ordered to leave all his birds, his books, and other personal property behind. That personal property had amounted to quite a lot. It weighed 1,144 pounds and filled five containers. It included, among other things, 30 empty birdcages, 158 bottles, cans, boxes and beakers of chemicals, and laboratory equipment. There were about 250 bird magazines, over 20 books on chemistry and microscopes, and many other catalogs and medical books. There were 85 pounds of various seeds, 118 feeding dishes, and 22 birds. In prison on a rocky island in San Francisco Bay, Stroud was **deprived** of all of this.

8   He turned then to the study of law and wrote an unpublished book on federal prison **reform**. He became known as the "Birdman of Alcatraz." He was the subject of newspaper and magazine articles, a book, and a movie.

9   The "Birdman" was kept in isolation for 42 years, longer than any federal prisoner in history. In 1959, in poor health but still **seeking parole,** he was transferred to the Federal Medical Center in Springfield, Missouri, where he died four years later. He had spent 56 years in prison.

VOCABULARY

What is the meaning of the underlined words? Circle the letter of the correct answer. Use a dictionary to check your answers.

1. Robert Stroud was said to be a cold and <u>vicious</u> man.

    a. cruel with a desire to hurt

    b. insane

    c. moody

2. People said that Robert Stroud should be <u>executed</u>.

    a. put in prison

    b. killed as lawful punishment

    c. sent to another country

3. Stroud was <u>sentenced</u> to 12 years in prison.

    a. recognized

    b. given admission

    c. given a punishment

4. Stroud <u>stabbed</u> a prisoner.

    a. poisoned

    b. strangled with his hands

    c. struck with a pointed weapon

5. Stroud's sentence was changed to life in <u>solitary confinement</u>.

    a. kept in prison for the rest of his life

    b. kept completely alone in prison

    c. kept in prison and made to work

6. Stroud became interested in <u>ornithology</u>.

    a. the study of diseases

    b. the study of birds

    c. the study of animals

7. His articles on birds were <u>smuggled out</u> of prison and published.

    a. removed legally

    b. transferred

    c. taken out illegally

8. In Alcatraz, Stroud was <u>deprived</u> of all his personal property.

    a. prevented from using

    b. delayed from using

    c. thinking of using

9. Stroud began to study law and wrote a book on prison <u>reform</u>.

    a. improvements in conditions

    b. organization of prisoners

    c. violence in prison

10. In 1959 Stroud was still <u>seeking parole</u>.

    a. asking to be tried again

    b. asking to be forgiven for his crimes

    c. asking to be let out of prison for good behavior

COMPREHENSION

A. Skimming for Main Ideas

Circle the letter of the best answer.

1. The main topic of Paragraph 4 is that
   a. Stroud killed a prison guard and almost died for it.
   b. Stroud had a very bad temper.
   c. Stroud's mother came to the aid of her son by petitioning the president.

2. Paragraph 5 is mainly about
   a. how Stroud found two baby birds.
   b. the beginning of Stroud's interest in birds.
   c. Stroud's kindness to animals.

3. The main topic of Paragraph 6 is that
   a. Stroud became an expert on bird diseases.
   b. Stroud became known for his canaries.
   c. Stroud wanted to be released.

4. Paragraph 7 is mainly about the fact that
   a. Stroud had to leave his birds behind.
   b. Stroud was sent to Alcatraz unfairly.
   c. Stroud was transferred to Alcatraz without his belongings.

B. Scanning for Details

Find the details to complete these sentences as quickly as possible. It is not necessary to read the whole passage again.

1. While Robert Stroud was in prison, he received diplomas from _____ University.

2. After Robert Stroud killed a man in Juneau, Alaska, he was sentenced to _____ years in _____ Prison.

3. While in prison Stroud cared for and studied _____.

4. Robert Stroud's studies while in prison earned him diplomas in the areas of

   _____ , _____ ,

   _____ , and theology.

5. Before he went to prison, Stroud had only received a

   _____ education.

6. When Stroud was transferred to Alcatraz, he had to leave behind

_____ .

7. After Stroud killed a guard and was sentenced to hang, his _____

asked President _____ to let him live.

8. Alcatraz Prison was located

_____ .

9. Instead of being hanged for his crime, Robert Stroud was given a sentence of

_____ .

10. In 1942 Stroud published a book on _____
that was considered the best work in the field.

C. Order of Events

Number the sentences to show the correct order.

_____ Stroud started taking correspondence courses.

_____ Stroud was sent to a prison in Washington state.

_____ Stroud was transferred to Alcatraz.

_____ Stroud killed a man in a dispute over a dance-hall girl.

_____ Stroud was transferred to Leavenworth Prison in Kansas.

_____ Stroud became interested in ornithology.

_____ Stroud became famous as the "Birdman of Alcatraz."

D. Making Inferences and Drawing Conclusions

The answers to these questions are not directly stated in the passage. Circle the letter of the best answer.

1. From the passage, it can be concluded that

   a. some people believed that Stroud should be set free.

   b. Stroud became famous because of the crimes he committed.

   c. President Wilson showed no pity toward Stroud and his mother.

2. It can be inferred from the passage that

  a. from the time of his first imprisonment, Stroud never had another chance to be free.

  b. Stroud was well treated by prison officials at Leavenworth.

  c. Stroud probably didn't mind being transferred to Alcatraz.

3. The passage implies that

  a. in spite of his lack of childhood education, Stroud proved to be highly intelligent.

  b. Stroud got along better with people than with animals.

  c. Stroud's transfer to Alcatraz made him completely lose interest in life.

DISCUSSION

Discuss the answers to these questions with your classmates.

1. Do you think prisoners should be allowed to study and get degrees in prison? Give your reasons.

2. How are crimes punished differently in different countries?

3. Do you think laws are too easy on criminals today?

4. Do you think the "Birdman" was treated fairly?

WRITING

Composition: State two reasons for and two reasons against capital punishment (execution for a crime).

RESEARCH

Below is a list of famous criminals. Find out what crime(s) each committed and how he or she died.

1. Al "Scarface" Capone

2. Jesse James

3. William H. Bonney ("Billy the Kid")

4. Albert di Salvo

5. John Dillinger

6. Ma Barker

BABE RUTH

Unit 6

Do you like baseball?

What famous baseball players do you know about?

Do people play baseball in your country?

1   George Herman Ruth was a poor boy who became a king. He was known as "The Babe" to millions of fans. He was one of America's greatest athletes and probably the most famous baseball player in the history of the sport. Ruth was baseball's "Home-Run King." He was a friendly, kind, often mischievous, and very generous man who won the hearts of millions of people around the world.

2   Babe Ruth was born to very poor parents in Baltimore, Maryland. Sometimes Babe and his sister didn't have food to eat. As Babe grew up he often got into trouble and was even caught stealing once. Before he turned eight years old, his parents put him into a school for problem children, St. Mary's Industrial School for Boys. One of the teachers, Brother Matthias, encouraged Babe to join the school's baseball team. By the time he was 16, he was the school's best **pitcher** and star player. Everyone loved to watch Babe play. They had no idea of the great **contribution** he would make to the sport of baseball.

3   When he was 19 and still at St. Mary's, Babe was offered a contract with the Baltimore Orioles. It is said that because of his youth and gentle personality, his teammates called him "Babe." It was a nickname that stuck for life. Babe pitched for the Orioles. Then he played as a pitcher and outfielder for the Boston Red Sox. He helped them win two World Series games. While Babe was an extraordinary pitcher, he was also developing a **reputation** as a powerful left-handed hitter. In 1919 he made his first record by hitting 29 **home runs** in one season, more than any previous **major-league** player.

4   In 1920 he was signed by the New York Yankees for what was then a record sum of money. The Yankees got more than they ever expected. Babe helped them win one World Series game after another. In the process, he became world famous as a home-run hitter. In 1923 he earned the American League's Most Valuable Player award. But it was the 1927 season that established Babe Ruth as the Home-Run King. On September 30 he hit home run number 60, which put him in the history books. No other baseball player had ever hit so many homers.

5   After that, sports fans **jammed** the stadiums just to see Babe Ruth play. One of Babe's most famous moments came during the 1932 World Series when the game was tied four-to-four. After two strikes, Ruth hit the longest home run that had ever been hit in Chicago's Wrigley Field. One story has it that Babe pointed to a spot in center field before hitting his powerful homer.

6   Babe Ruth inspired legends, but more importantly, his determination and love of the sport changed baseball forever. Interest in baseball at home and abroad **soared**. Players' salaries increased. Babe became one of the first real sports stars of the 20th century. When he retired, he had been at bat 8,399 times and had hit 714 home runs. He was the greatest baseball player who ever lived.

7   Although today some of Ruth's records have been broken, Babe's personality and his influence on the game of baseball are unmatched. He brought fun, excitement, and **renown** to the sport. Just as in his youth, Ruth's high spirits got him into trouble on occasion. He got into fights, got tickets for speeding, and went to lots of parties. Once he was even **suspended** from playing for a short while because of his bad behavior at a game. Nevertheless, everyone knew that he was a kind and sensitive man who understood and accepted the responsibility he had to his fans, particularly the children. He never forgot his difficult youth. Letters from children always received Babe's attention. He sent out thousands of autographed pictures to boys and girls who asked for them. He also made countless free appearances for charity. In 1947 he started the Babe Ruth Foundation, an organization that helped **underprivileged** children. When he died in 1948, he left behind a reputation not only as a great sportsman but as a great man as well.

VOCABULARY

Complete each definition with one of the following words. Guess your answers, then check with a dictionary.

pitcher	contribution	major-league	renown
home run	reputation	jammed	
soared	suspended	underprivileged	

1. When a person helps to make something better, he or she makes a

   _____ .

2. When a place is _____ , it is tightly packed by a crowd of people.

3. When something went up high or rose very fast it _____ .

4. When people do not have the advantages of other people, they are

   _____ .

5. When a person is prevented from belonging to a group for a period of time, usually

   because of bad behavior, he or she is _____ .

6. Another word for *fame* is _____ .

7. The recognition by others of some characteristic or ability is a

   _____ .

8. In baseball, the player who throws the ball toward the person who is going to hit it is

   the _____ .

9. In baseball, when a player hits the ball and goes around all the bases and scores a

   point, it is a _____ .

10. A league of the highest classification in U.S. professional baseball is

   _____ .

COMPREHENSION

A. Skimming for Main Ideas

Circle the letter of the best answer.

1. Paragraph 2 is mainly about
   a. Babe's childhood and beginning in baseball.
   b. how Brother Matthias encouraged Babe.
   c. why Babe was a problem child.

2. The main topic in Paragraph 3 is that
   a. Babe played for the Baltimore Orioles.
   b. Babe started his career in professional baseball.
   c. Babe broke a record.

3. The main topic in Paragraph 6 is that
   a. Babe became one of the first sports stars of the century.
   b. Babe increased interest in baseball around the world.
   c. Babe made a great contribution to the game of baseball.

4. The last paragraph is mainly about
   a. Babe's bad behavior at games.
   b. Babe's personality and reputation.
   c. Babe's foundation for underprivileged children.

B. Scanning for Details

Scan the paragraphs for details. It is not necessary to read the whole passage again. Circle T if the statement is true. Circle F if the statement is false.

1. On September 30, 1927, Babe Ruth broke a record by hitting his 60th home run.   T   F

2. Babe Ruth was known as the "Home-Run King."   T   F

3. Babe Ruth started playing baseball when he was eight years old.   T   F

4. The first baseball team Babe Ruth played with was the Boston Red Sox.   T   F

5. Babe Ruth started his baseball career as a hitter.   T   F

6. Ruth helped the Boston Red Sox win two World Series games.   T   F

7. Babe Ruth was playing for the Baltimore Orioles when he got his first Most Valuable Player award.   T   F

8. Babe Ruth was one of the first sports stars of the 20th century.   T   F

9. Babe Ruth's hitting records have never been broken.   T   F

10. Many fans went to the baseball games just to see Babe Ruth play.   T   F

C. Order of Events

Number the sentences to show the correct order.

_____ Babe Ruth hit the longest home run ever hit in Wrigley Field.

_____ Babe Ruth joined the baseball team at St. Mary's Industrial School for Boys.

_____ Babe Ruth hit 29 home runs while playing for the Red Sox.

_____ Babe Ruth was put into a school for problem children.

_____ Babe Ruth was signed by the New York Yankees.

_____ Babe Ruth broke an all-time record of 60 home runs.

_____ Babe pitched for the Baltimore Orioles.

D. Making Inferences and Drawing Conclusions

The answers to these questions are not directly stated in the passage. Circle the letter of the best answer.

1. From the passage, it can be concluded that
   a. Babe Ruth's ability to play baseball saved him from a difficult and troubled life.
   b. Babe Ruth's ability to succeed could be seen from the time he was a child.
   c. Babe Ruth was asked to join the school team because everyone knew he would one day be a star athlete.

2. It can be inferred from the passage that
   a. Babe Ruth's bad behavior made his fans dislike him.
   b. Babe Ruth's personality added to his success as an athlete.
   c. Babe Ruth never thought about his poor and troubled childhood once he became a baseball star.

3. The passage implies that
   a. Babe Ruth's greatest contribution to baseball was attracting interest in the sport worldwide.
   b. By the time he retired, fans no longer had much interest in Babe Ruth.
   c. Babe Ruth established the Babe Ruth Foundation so people would remember him.

DISCUSSION

Discuss the answers to these questions with your classmates.

1. Do you think men and women will ever play professional baseball on the same team?

2. Who is the most popular sports star in your country? Why is he or she so popular?

3. What do you think would have happened to Babe Ruth if he had never played baseball?

4. Babe Ruth started a foundation for underprivileged children. Do you think sports stars have an obligation to give something back to the community?

WRITING

Composition: Sports have been played as far back as primitive man. Why have sports always been so important to people? Give reasons with examples.

RESEARCH

Find out which sport each of the following athletes is associated with.

1. Hank Aaron
2. Sonja Henie
3. Chris Evert
4. Wayne Gretzky
5. Joe Louis
6. Oscar Robertson
7. Willie Shoemaker
8. Jack Nicklaus

PLACES

Part 2

Unit 7

Alaska—The Last Frontier

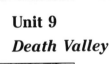

Unit 8

The Mystery of Roanoke Island

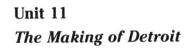

Unit 9

Death Valley

Unit 10

The Okefenokee

Unit 11

The Making of Detroit

ALASKA— THE LAST FRONTIER

*Look at the pictures of the animals.
Which ones are found in your country?*

What do you know about Alaska?

*Would you like to live there? Why or
why not?*

1   There is nothing small or ordinary about Alaska. It is America's largest state. It has the highest mountain and the largest glacier in North America. Its chain of volcanoes is the longest in the world. It has vast regions of uninhabited land richly diverse in both geography and wildlife. It is a remarkable place known as the "Last Frontier."

2   Alaska fits its name very well. It comes from the word *alyeska*, meaning "Great Land" in the language of its native Aleut people. Alaska covers 591,004 square miles. Rhode Island would fit into Alaska 480 times! The highest point in Alaska is 20,320-foot Mount McKinley. The 16 highest mountains in the United

States are all in Alaska. There are also about 100,000 glaciers. The largest, Malaspina Glacier, covers 850 square miles. Alaska also has more than three million lakes and 3,000 rivers, much more than any other state.

3   Everything about Alaska seems to be big. The largest salmon **on record** was caught in 1985 in Alaska's Kenia River. It weighed 97 pounds, 4 ounces. Its brown bears, called Kodiak bears, are the world's largest bears. Even the vegetables grown there are big. Cabbages have been known to weigh 95 pounds and carrots to be 3 feet long! If you took a trip through Alaska, it would take quite a long while to cover its **vast** territory. You'd have to take an airplane from place to place because much of Alaska doesn't have roads.

4   Along the coast you would see thousands of islands, rocks, and **reefs**. You'd see glaciers and icebergs, which are huge pieces of glaciers that fall into the water. Glaciers cover nearly 29,000 square miles of Alaska. Most are in the south and southeast.

5   In south-central Alaska, you'd fly over the Alaskan Mountain **Range** and Mount McKinley. Thousands of visitors have climbed up Mount McKinley. Others have died trying. The youngest person to climb Mount McKinley was Taras Genet of Talkeetna, Alaska, who climbed it in 1991 when he was 12 years old.

6   No doubt you would visit several of Alaska's national parks. In these protected lands there are glaciers, mountains, active volcanoes, lakes, rivers, forests, and wildlife of many kinds. Besides Kodiak bears, there are grizzly bears, polar bears, moose, caribou, wolves, porcupines, beavers, mountain goats, foxes, and squirrels. Alaska has 450 kinds of birds. In its waters, whales and dolphins swim along the coast. Seals, walruses, and sea otters are also found there.

7   Part of Alaska lies within the Arctic Circle. The land there is called *tundra*. There are no trees because the soil is permanently frozen. This frozen soil, called *permafrost*, **thaws** on the surface during the summer, when it is covered with a thick layer of **mosses**, wildflowers, and grasses. People who live there have a special problem because of the permafrost. A house built on it sometimes causes it to thaw beneath the house. The thawed soil begins to sink down, and the house goes with it! Many arctic inhabitants build their houses on platforms so they can be moved from time to time.

8   If you lived in the arctic, you would know why Alaska is also called the "Land of the Midnight Sun." At Barrow, the northernmost point, the sun does not set from May 10 to August 2. There is daylight all that time. But from November 18 to January 24, Barrow has no sunlight. Then the average temperature is minus 11 degrees Fahrenheit. If you went to the arctic in the spring and autumn you'd see the northern lights. This is a **natural phenomenon** in which the night skies are filled with **spectacular** colors, also called the aurora borealis.

9   Alaska is a very different and special place, and so are its people. Alaska has a very small population for such a big place. Many Alaskan towns have fewer than 100 residents. One such town is Chicken, which has a population of 37. Many towns, like Chicken, have unusual names, such as Clam Gulch, Candle, Beaver, Deadhorse, King Salmon, and Eek. Many were named by the adventurous and often **eccentric** prospectors who came to Alaska looking for gold in the 1800s.

10   Most Alaskans live in the cities, such as Anchorage, Fairbanks, and Juneau, where there is work and a modern way of life. The population of Alaska is growing rapidly, and today about two-thirds of Alaskans were born elsewhere. They come from many countries to work in the oil, mining, **timber**, and fishing industries.

11   Native-born Alaskans include both native peoples and the descendants of the early settlers. The natives, which are the Eskimos, Aleuts, and Indians, migrated to Alaska from Siberia as far back as 15,000 years ago. Some of the natives still live the way their ancestors did, hunting and fishing in the wilderness. Others have modern lives in the cities. However, no matter where they live or when they got there or what ethnic group they belong to, all Alaskans have one thing in common. That is the splendors of the great land in which they live.

VOCABULARY

Complete each definition with one of the following words or phrases. Guess your answers, then check with a dictionary.

on record	vast	thaws	natural phenomenon
reefs	range	mosses	
spectacular	timber	eccentric	

1. _____ is wood or trees grown for use in building.

2. _____ people are strange and behave in an unusual manner.

3. Facts or events _____ are written down and preserved.

4. Something great in size is _____ .

5. _____ are lines of rocks or sand near the surface of the sea.

6. When something frozen becomes soft or liquid it _____ .

7. _____ are small, flat, green or yellow plants without flowers that grow like a thin carpet on wet soil.

8. A connected line or chain of mountains is a _____ .

9. Something _____ is sensational and striking to watch.

10. An unusual event in nature is a _____ .

COMPREHENSION

A. Skimming for Main Ideas

Circle the letter of the best answer.

1. Paragraph 3 is mainly about the fact that
   a. Alaska covers an enormous area.
   b. everything in Alaska is big.
   c. vegetables that grow in Alaska are big.

2. Paragraph 7 is mainly about
   a. the characteristics of the tundra.
   b. when summer comes to the tundra.
   c. the people who live in the tundra.

3. Paragraph 8 mostly discusses the fact that
   a. spring is the best time to visit Alaska.
   b. the northern lights are a natural phenomenon.
   c. Alaska is known as the "Land of the Midnight Sun."

4. The last paragraph is mainly about
   a. native peoples and descendants of the early settlers who make up the native-born Alaskans.
   b. the native peoples who still live the ways their ancestors did.
   c. native-born Alaskans who live in big cities today.

B. Scanning for Details

Find the details to complete these sentences as quickly as possible. It is not necessary to read the whole passage again.

1. Alaska means _____ in the language of its native

   _____ people.

2. Alaska's brown bears, called _____ bears, are the largest bears in the world.

3. The treeless land within the Arctic Circle is called _____ .

4. Because the sun does not set during summer in the northernmost regions, Alaska is

   also called _____ .

5. Native-born Alaskans include both _____ and

_____ .

6. The highest point in Alaska is _____ , which is

_____ feet high.

7. The colors that can be seen in the night skies in autumn are called the

_____ or _____ .

8. In Alaska there are about _____ glaciers, three million lakes, and

_____ rivers.

9. The best way to travel across Alaska is by _____ because

_____ .

10. The native people of Alaska migrated from _____ .

C. Order of Events

Number the sentences to show the correct order.

_____ Taras Genet climbed Mount McKinley.

_____ Prospectors came to Alaska looking for gold.

_____ Eskimos, Aleuts, and Indians migrated to Alaska.

_____ The largest salmon on record was caught in the Kenia River.

D. Making Inferences and Drawing Conclusions

The answers to these questions are not directly stated in the passage. Circle the letter of the best answer.

1. From the passage, it can be concluded that

  a. all Alaskans travel by plane.

  b. traveling through Alaska on foot would be difficult and dangerous.

  c. because most of Alaska is wilderness, there isn't much for visitors to see there.

2. It can be inferred from the passage that

  a. it is impossible for people to live in the area within the Arctic Circle.

  b. the native Alaskans have lost their ability to survive in the wilderness.

  c. the majority of Alaska's population are immigrants living in urban areas.

3. The passage implies that

    a. people who live in Alaska must learn to live in the wilderness.

    b. Alaska's native people adapted to the harsh climate and made use of natural resources.

    c. most of the prospectors who went to Alaska looking for gold didn't stay there.

DISCUSSION

Discuss the answers to these questions with your classmates.

1. Some people in Alaska live alone in the wilderness. Discuss the pros and cons of living this way.

2. Do you believe that native peoples should leave their traditional ways of life and live in a modern society?

3. What area of your country is considered very beautiful? Compare it with Alaska.

4. Some people like to live in a cold climate. Others like it hot. What is your favorite climate to live in? How do you think climate affects the way people live?

WRITING

Composition: Compare and contrast two different types of houses that are found in different environments. Explain how the building materials and styles are meant to adapt to each environment.

RESEARCH

Find the following facts about Alaska.

1. Population   **3.** Festivals   **5.** Agriculture

2. National parks   **4.** Minerals   **6.** Fishing

THE MYSTERY OF ROANOKE ISLAND

Do you like mysteries? Why?

What mysterious places do you know?

*What people do you know whose life or
death involves mystery?*

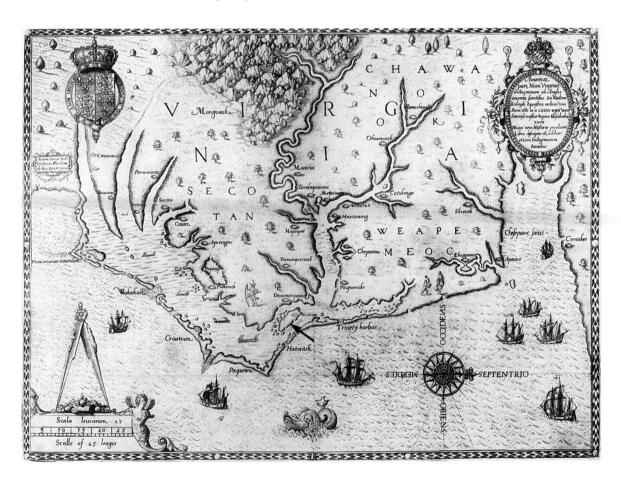

1   Everyone loves a mystery. Books, stories, movies, and television programs
involving mysteries are very popular. Fictional mysteries are fun to try to solve
before the author finally reveals the secret. However, there are many real-life
mysteries that have never been solved. One of them is the mystery of the
"Lost Colony" of Roanoke.

2   The story begins in 1585. An English explorer named Sir Walter Raleigh
wanted to start settlements in the New World for his glory and that of his
queen, Elizabeth I. Raleigh sent 108 men to settle on Roanoke Island, off the

coast of Virginia*. However, these men were soldiers and didn't know how to farm. They quickly ran out of food. By 1586 the settlers were sick and starving.

3   One day some English ships **anchored** near the island. The captains of these ships agreed to take the settlers back to England. The settlers brought back with them Indian corn and potatoes, which were unknown in England. Sir Walter Raleigh planted the potatoes on his estate in Ireland. Later they became a chief source of food for the Irish people.

4   Raleigh was still determined to start a colony in Virginia. This time he decided to include farmers and families who could build things and survive in their settlement. In 1587 he sent 150 men, women, and children in three ships across the sea. Many had sold everything they owned in hopes of a better life in the New World. The ships were on their way to Chesapeake Bay, where it was thought a settlement could be more successful than on Roanoke Island. However, the ships' captain stopped at Roanoke and refused to take his passengers any farther. They had no choice but to settle on the island.

5   They repaired the old **fort** and began to build cabins. But they soon realized they would need many more supplies than they had brought with them. It was decided that their leader and governor, John White, should go back to England for help and more **provisions**. A week before he sailed, White's daughter gave birth to a baby girl—the first English child to be born in America. Her name was Virginia Dare. As conditions on the island were difficult, some of the settlers wanted to move to another place. Before Governor White left, he told them that if they left the island, they should **carve** on a tree the name of the place where they were going. If they had troubles, they should put a cross above the name.

6   Upon reaching England, White discovered that England was at war with Spain. Every ship in the country was needed. He and Sir Walter Raleigh tried in every way to send ships to the **stranded** little colony across the sea. But it was not to be. Three years passed before White was able to return to Roanoke Island.

7   In August of 1590, the governor stepped ashore at Roanoke. He walked to the settlement with fear in his heart. Upon reaching it, he found only **deserted ruins**. The cabins had been destroyed and the ground was overgrown with high grass and weeds. He found rusted pieces of metal and **moldy** books. It was obvious the colony had been **abandoned** for at least a year.

8   White was deeply troubled. But then, at the entrance to the settlement, he saw the word *CROATOAN* carved in a tree. There was no cross above the word. Croatoan was the name of a nearby island inhabited by a friendly native tribe. White was confident the settlers would be found.

9   The ship's captain agreed to sail to Croatoan the next morning. But during the night, there was a terrible storm. The ship lost all but one anchor. The captain was more concerned for his ship than for the colonists, so he sailed away from the storm. But the storm followed and blew them far into the Atlantic. The captain refused to go back, so White unhappily was taken back to England.

10   Although several search parties were eventually sent to Roanoke and Croatoan, not one clue to the fate of the settlers was ever found. Governor

*__Virginia:__ In 1585 Virginia was a region much larger than the present state of the same name. Nowadays, Roanoke Island is in the state of North Carolina.

White would never know what happened to his daughter and grandchild, or all the others who had so bravely made the journey with him.

11   **Ironically**, the fate of Governor White also became a mystery. It is not known where or when he died. There is a record that in 1606 a man named John White died "in parts beyond the sea." It seems very likely that White died still searching for the men and women he had left with a promise of help, but was unable to save.

VOCABULARY

What is the meaning of the underlined words? Circle the letter of the correct answer. Use a dictionary to check your answers.

1. Some English ships <u>anchored</u> near Roanoke Island.

   a. were unable to sail because there was no wind

   b. hit upon some rocks and then repaired the ships

   c. stayed in one place by putting out a rope with a piece of metal at the end

2. The settlers repaired the old <u>fort</u>.

   a. strongly-made building used for defense

   b. roughly-made religious building

   c. strongly-made bridge

3. John White went back to England for help and <u>provisions</u>.

   a. settlers

   b. soldiers

   c. supplies

4. He told them to <u>carve</u> the name of their destination on a tree.

   a. cut

   b. paint

   c. attach

5. They tried to send ships to the <u>stranded</u> colony across the sea.

   a. created for a special purpose

   b. left in a helpless position

   c. populated by a few people

6. The governor found <u>deserted</u> ruins.

   a. dried up

   b. left empty

   c. ancient

7. He found <u>ruins</u>.

   a. household objects

   b. remains of buildings

   c. uncared for fields

8. The colony had been <u>abandoned</u> for at least a year.

   a. left completely and forever

   b. left temporarily

   c. occupied

9. The books were <u>moldy</u>.

    a. covered with a greenish growth

    b. filled with pictures

    c. dried up

10. <u>Ironically</u>, the fate of Governor White became a mystery too.

    a. contradictorily

    b. unfortunately

    c. interestingly

COMPREHENSION

A. Skimming for Main Ideas

Circle the letter of the best answer.

1. The main topic of Paragraph 4 is

    a. Raleigh made the decision to start a colony in Virginia.

    b. why people sold everything they owned.

    c. why farmers were needed in the colony.

2. The main topic of Paragraph 7 is

    a. the governor became afraid at Roanoke.

    b. the governor found Roanoke deserted.

    c. the settlement was overgrown with grass.

3. Paragraph 10 is mainly about

    a. what the search parties found at Roanoke.

    b. no one knowing what happened to the settlers.

    c. the governor's search for his daughter.

4. The main topic of the last paragraph is

    a. the mystery of what happened to Governor White.

    b. the death of Governor White at sea.

    c. White's search for the men and women at Roanoke.

B. Scanning for Details

Scan the paragraphs for details. It is not necessary to read the whole passage again. Circle T if the statement is true. Circle F if the statement is false.

1. Governor White's granddaughter was the first English child born in America.   T   F

2. The first settlers on Roanoke did not have the skills to survive in the wilderness.   T   F

3. Governor White left Roanoke because he wanted to go fight for the British Navy.   **T**   **F**

4. Governor White couldn't return to Roanoke because Sir Walter Raleigh had lost interest in the colony.   **T**   **F**

5. It was five years before Governor White could return to Roanoke.   **T**   **F**

6. Sir Walter Raleigh was mostly interested in importing plants from the New World.   **T**   **F**

7. Most of the colonists went to Roanoke with the intention of eventually returning to England.   **T**   **F**

8. The colonists left a message saying where they had gone.   **T**   **F**

9. Governor White died a lonely death in England.   **T**   **F**

10. When Governor White finally returned to Roanoke, he found all the buildings still standing, but the colonists were no longer there.   **T**   **F**

C. Order of Events

Number the sentences to show the correct order.

_____ The settlers needed more supplies for the colony.

_____ Governor White found the remains of the settlement.

_____ Sir Walter Raleigh sent 108 men to settle on Roanoke.

_____ Three ships brought settler families to Roanoke.

_____ Search parties were sent to find the missing colonists.

_____ Indian corn and potatoes were taken to England and Ireland.

_____ Governor White left for England.

D. Making Inferences and Drawing Conclusions

The answers to these questions are not directly stated in the passage. Circle the letter of the best answer.

1. From the passage, it can be concluded that

   a. Roanoke Island was not the best place to try to start a colony.

   b. Roanoke Island was rich in natural resources.

   c. it wasn't necessary for Governor White to leave Roanoke.

2. It can be inferred from the passage that

   a. Governor White didn't like Sir Walter Raleigh.

   b. Governor White was not planning to return to the colony after he left.

   c. Governor White didn't think the colony could survive without more supplies.

3. The passage implies that

   a. if Governor White had stayed on Roanoke, the colony would have been a success.

   b. storms probably drove the colonists off Roanoke.

   c. when the colonists left Roanoke, they were probably not in danger.

DISCUSSION

Discuss the answers to these questions with your classmates.

1. Do you think Governor White should have left the settlers on the island?

2. What do you think happened to Governor White?

3. There are many mysteries concerning outer space. Do you believe there is life on other planets? Do you think other beings or aliens have visited earth?

4. Do you believe in spirits? Give reasons.

WRITING

Composition: Continue the story of Roanoke. Write what you think happened to the settlers. Give at least one reason for your opinion.

RESEARCH

Choose one of the following mysteries. Find out when, where, and what the mystery is.

1. The Bermuda Triangle

2. The statues on Easter Island

3. The Nazca lines

4. Atlantis

DEATH VALLEY

Unit 9

Where do you think some of the hottest and coldest places in the world are located?

How do you think Death Valley got its name?

Would you like to visit a place that is either extremely hot or extremely cold? Why?

1   Death Valley doesn't sound like a very inviting place. It is one of the hottest places in the world. The highest temperature ever recorded there was 134 degrees Fahrenheit. That is the highest ever recorded in the Western Hemisphere. And that was in the shade! Death Valley in California covers nearly 3,000 square miles. Approximately 555 square miles are below the surface of the sea. One point is 282 feet below sea level—the lowest point in the Western Hemisphere. In Death Valley, **pioneers** and explorers faced death from thirst and the **searing** heat. Yet despite its name and bad reputation, Death Valley is not just an empty wilderness of sand and rock. It is a place of spectacular scenic beauty and home to plants, animals, and even humans.

2   In 1849 a small group of pioneers struggled for three months to get across the rough land. They suffered great hardships as they and their wagons traveled slowly across the **salt flats** in the baking sun. They ran out of food and

DEATH VALLEY   *53*

had to eat the oxen and leave their possessions behind. They ran out of water and became so thirsty they could not swallow the meat. They found a lake and fell on their knees, only to discover it was heavily salted. Finally, weak and reduced to almost skeletons, they came upon a spring of fresh water and their lives were saved. When they finally reached the mountains on the other side, they slowly climbed up the rocky slopes. One of them looked back and said, "Goodbye, Death Valley." That has been its name ever since.

3   Death Valley is the driest place in North America. Yet far from being dead, it is alive with plants and animals. They have adapted to this **harsh** region. In the salt flats on the valley floor, there are no plants to be seen. But near the edge, there are grasses. Farther away, there are some small bushes and cactus. On higher ground there are **shrubs** and shrub-like trees. Finally, high on the mountainside, there are pine trees.

4   What is not visible are the seeds **lodged** in the soil, waiting for rain. When it does come, a brilliant display of flowers carpets the once barren flatlands. Even the cactus blossoms. It is the most common of all desert plants. As the water dries up and the hot summer nears, the flowers die. But first they produce seeds that will wait for the rains of another year.

5   At noon on a summer day, Death Valley looks truly **devoid of** wildlife. But in reality, there are 55 species of mammals, 32 kinds of birds, 36 kinds of reptiles, and 3 kinds of **amphibians**. During the day many seek shelter under rocks and in **burrows**. As night approaches, however, the land cools. The desert becomes a center of animal activity. Owls hunt for mice. Bats gather insects as they fly. The little kit fox is out looking for food, accompanied by snakes, hawks, coyotes, and bobcats. Many of these animals, like the desert plants, have adapted to the dry desert. They use water very efficiently. They can often survive on water supplies that would leave similar animals elsewhere dying of thirst.

6   Humans have also learned how to survive in this land. Little is known about the first people, the Lake Mohave people, except that they hunted there as long as 9,000 years ago. From 5,000 to 2,000 years ago, the Mesquite Flat people inhabited the region. Then the Saratoga people came. Finally, about 1,000 years ago, the earliest of the Shoshone natives moved in. To this day, a few Shoshone families live the winter months in the desert.

7   The natives knew where every hidden spring was. They also knew the habits of the desert animals, which they hunted. The natives, and later even the prospectors, ate every imaginable desert animal. They ate everything from the bighorn sheep to snakes, rats, and lizards. They were often on the edge of starvation. In autumn they gathered nuts from the pine trees. Other foods they ate included roots, cactus plants, leaves, and sometimes insects.

8   The early prospectors didn't know the desert as well as the natives. Many died looking for gold and silver in Death Valley. Others did find the **precious** metals. Then a "boomtown" was born. First it consisted of miners living in tents. Then permanent buildings were built. But when the mine failed, the town that built up around it did too. Today the remains of these "ghost towns" are scattered about Death Valley. They have names like Skidoo, Panamint City, Chloride City, and Greenwater.

9   Going to Death Valley once meant danger, hardship, and even death. Today, visitors can drive there in air-conditioned comfort. They can stay in hotels. They don't have to worry about dying of hunger or thirst. They can look upon the hills, canyons, and cactus with appreciation rather than fear. They can admire the beauty of this strange land. They can leave with happy memories.

VOCABULARY

Complete each definition with one of the following words or phrases. Guess your answers, then check with a dictionary.

pioneers	searing	devoid of	shrubs
salt flats	harsh	burrows	
lodged	amphibians	precious	

1. Animals that can live both on land and in water are _____ .

2. _____ are holes in the ground made by animals and in which the animals live.

3. Intense heat that almost burns is _____ .

4. _____ are flat areas covered with salt as a result of water that had been there some time ago and then evaporated.

5. _____ are low bushes.

6. To be _____ something means to be empty of.

7. _____ means severe and rough.

8. _____ are the first settlers in a new or unknown land.

9. Rare and valuable metals such as gold and silver are _____ metals.

10. To be planted firmly or embedded is to be _____ .

COMPREHENSION

A. Skimming for Main Ideas

Circle the letter of the best answer.

1. The main topic of Paragraph 2 is
   a. the hardships a small group of pioneers suffered in Death Valley.
   b. people have always avoided Death Valley.
   c. some places in Death Valley are covered with salt.

2. Paragraph 5 is mainly about the fact that
   a. Death Valley is a place full of wildlife.
   b. many kinds of reptiles live in Death Valley.
   c. the animals that live in Death Valley live on desert plants.

3. The main topic of Paragraph 6 is
   a. the Lake Mohave people were the earliest and only people who lived in Death Valley.
   b. many peoples have learned to survive in Death Valley.
   c. many native tribes live in Death Valley today.

4. The last paragraph is mainly about
   a. the dangers of going to Death Valley today.
   b. how nature has changed in Death Valley today.
   c. what Death Valley is like for visitors today.

B. Scanning for Details

Find the details as quickly as possible and circle the letter of the correct answer. It is not necessary to read the whole passage again.

1. For the early pioneers, crossing Death Valley took as long as
   a. one year.
   b. six months.
   c. three months.

2. Rain in Death Valley causes
   a. flowers to bloom.
   b. minerals to form.
   c. animals to come out and hunt.

3. When prospectors found gold, it often caused
   a. hardship for them.
   b. the soil to be eroded.
   c. a town to be created.

4. Death Valley got its name from
   a. the natives who settled there.
   b. a group of settlers who almost died there.
   c. some prospectors who went there

5. Death Valley is home to plants and animals that have

   a. adapted to the environment.

   b. been brought there by humans.

   c. not been able to survive anyplace else.

6. Settlers could not drink from a lake in Death Valley because

   a. it was salty.

   b. it was empty.

   c. they couldn't reach it.

7. The first people to live in Death Valley were the

   a. Mesquite Flat people.

   b. Lake Mohave people.

   c. Shoshone natives.

8. Of all places in North America, Death Valley is the

   a. highest.

   b. driest.

   c. least populated.

9. The natives could survive in Death Valley because

   a. they didn't stay there all year.

   b. they brought food with them from the mountains.

   c. they knew the location of hidden water.

10. During the day most of the animals in Death Valley

   a. hunt.

   b. find shelter.

   c. eat desert plants.

C. Order of Events

Number the sentences to show the correct order.

_____ "Boomtowns" were created.

_____ The Saratoga people inhabited Death Valley.

_____ Some mines failed.

_____ The prospectors came looking for gold.

_____ "Ghost towns" were left scattered throughout the desert.

D. Making Inferences and Drawing Conclusions

The answers to these questions are not directly stated in the passage. Circle the letter of the best answer.

1. From the passage, it can be concluded that

   a. living things have an ability to adapt to the worst environments.

   b. the plants and animals of Death Valley will soon disappear.

   c. mammals make up the smallest part of Death Valley's wildlife population.

2. It can be inferred from the passage that

    a. people no longer live in Death Valley.

    b. the native peoples didn't settle for very long in Death Valley.

    c. although some prospectors died, others were resourceful enough to live in Death Valley.

3. The passage implies that

    a. most of the people who went to live in Death Valley died there.

    b. there are no reasons for anyone to go to Death Valley today.

    c. without gold, people found little reason to live in Death Valley.

DISCUSSION

Discuss the answers to these questions with your classmates.

1. Why do you think people choose to live in places that have harsh conditions?

2. What type of climate do you have in your country? How have the people there adapted to the climate?

3. If you had to survive on your own in Death Valley, how would you do it?

4. Do you think the world's climate is getting warmer? What do you think the effect of this climate change will be?

WRITING

Composition: Describe what you think would be the ideal place to live. Describe the climate and landscape and why you would like to live there.

RESEARCH

Find out what the climate is like in each of the following areas of the United States. Name at least two plants and two animals that can be found in each place.

1. Painted Desert, Arizona

2. The Everglades, Florida

3. Cape Cod, Massachusetts

4. The Badlands, South Dakota

5. The Rocky Mountains, Colorado

THE OKEFENOKEE

Unit 10

Look at the picture. What kind of place do you think this is?

What kind of animals do you think live here?

Do you think people could live in a place like this?

1   The mysterious, and once unknown and terrifying, Okefenokee Swamp is located in southeastern Georgia. It covers over 660 square miles. It is an ancient place with thick forests. The air is moist and heavy. There are narrow waterways and misty lakes full of water plants. Many animals live in the **swamp's** waters, on its islands, or high in its trees. For people, this jungle once served as a safe place to hide or as a home far away from civilization. Today, most of the swamp is a national wildlife **refuge**. The people have gone, but the beauty and mystery remain.

2   The Native Americans named the swamp Okefenokee (pronounced O-kee-fe-no-kee), from a native word meaning "Land of the Trembling Earth." That's

because on many of the smaller islands, the trees and plants shook when people walked on the ground. Some Native Americans hid in the swamp to get away from government soldiers who wanted to put them on reservations. Some eventually left but others stayed and made the swamp their home.

3   For most people the swamp was a dark, **enchanted** place. It was full of mystery, superstition, and danger. But there was a group of people who didn't see it that way. For them, it was a paradise of trees and animals and water. It was also a place where they could live isolated from the rest of the world. These people arrived in 1850. They were a small group of Georgia pioneers who made the swamp their home. Far from civilization, they developed a unique way of life. They had their own manners, customs, and speech, and became known as "swampers."

4   The swampers were a tough, **self-sufficient** people who lived a simple, almost primitive way of life. Yet in many ways they lived **carefree**, comfortable lives too. They lived on grassy, forested islands on which they built **sturdy** cabins and planted gardens. They fished and hunted for food. There were plenty of animals to hunt, such as deer, wild ducks, rabbits, wild turkeys, and squirrels. There were also dangerous animals such as bears, cougars, and alligators. Even though alligators are very dangerous, the swampers learned to catch them. A swamper would put a long stick into a deep pool where he thought an alligator lived. Holding one end of the pole between his teeth, he would imitate the animal's deep **growl**. Pretty soon, the alligator would come up to investigate. Then the swamper would shoot it. Swampers ate the alligator and made things with its skin.

5   As swampers seldom had books or newspapers, they developed the art of storytelling. They made up stories about the swamp and its creatures, and about their lives. They told them around the fireside, and these stories were passed from one generation to another. Music was also an important part of life in the swamp. Swampers sang folk songs, which are songs they made up about their lives. They often played their fiddles and banjos, and sang and danced. The swamp was very dark and thick with vegetation, so it was difficult for people to see each other. The swampers developed a way of communicating called "hollerin'." It was a type of yodel, or call, that could be heard for miles. Each person had a special holler that identified him to the others.

6   The swampers lived in peace in the Okefenokee until 1908 when a lumber company bought the swamp and covered it with railroad tracks. Then they came in and cut down hundreds of trees. They brought in hundreds of workers and built a small town on one of the largest islands. It had a bank and stores and even a movie theater. Six hundred people lived and worked there for 15 years. The wildlife were driven into the farthest parts of the swamp. The swampers, too, began to leave, although some worked for the lumber company. By 1935 all of the biggest trees were gone. The company left and the town was abandoned. The machinery rusted and the homes **decayed**. The grasses grew high, covering everything. The swamp eventually took back its land. But the swamp would never be the same again.

7   The state transferred the property to the federal government, and a wildlife **preserve** was created. It was already too late for some species, such as the ivory-billed woodpecker, which **became extinct**. But for hundreds of other plant and animal species it was their last hope of survival. Today, it is a safe hiding place, not for people, but for nature and its creatures.

VOCABULARY

What is the meaning of the underlined words? Circle the letter of the correct answer. Use a dictionary to check your answers.

1. Many animals live in the <u>swamp</u>.
   a. high land with forest
   b. large area of flat land
   c. soft, wet land

2. Most of the swamp is a wildlife <u>refuge</u>.
   a. a place that is safe from danger
   b. a place that is mysterious
   c. a place where nature is beautiful

3. For most people the swamp was an <u>enchanted</u> place.
   a. dangerous
   b. magical
   c. isolated

4. The swampers were <u>self-sufficient</u> people.
   a. wild and savage
   b. living without outside help
   c. very hardworking

5. The swampers lived <u>carefree</u> lives.
   a. untroubled
   b. convenient
   c. healthy

6. The swampers built <u>sturdy</u> cabins on the islands.
   a. rough
   b. small
   c. strong

7. The swamper would imitate the alligator's <u>growl</u>.
   a. rough, angry sound
   b. slow movements
   c. crying sound

8. After the town was abandoned, the homes <u>decayed</u>.
   a. disappeared completely
   b. fell down
   c. began to rot

9. The swamp was created into a wildlife <u>preserve</u> by the federal government.
   a. an area for private fishing
   b. an area used for hunting
   c. an area where nature and animals are protected

10. Some animal species <u>became extinct</u>.
    a. ended
    b. were undiscovered
    c. went far away

COMPREHENSION

A. Skimming for Main Ideas

Circle the letter of the best answer.

1. Paragraph 2 is mainly about

    a. the relationship the Native Americans had with the swamp.

    b. why the Native Americans hid in the swamp.

    c. what Okefenokee means.

2. The main topic of Paragraph 4 is

    a. how the swampers caught alligators.

    b. the simple and independent way of life the swampers had.

    c. what animals the swampers hunted.

3. The main topic of Paragraph 5 is

    a. the art of storytelling the swampers developed.

    b. the kind of music the swampers created and the instruments they used to play it.

    c. the special forms of art and communication developed by the swampers.

4. Paragraph 6 is mainly about

    a. what happened when the lumber company came to the swamp.

    b. the town the lumber company built.

    c. what happened when the lumber company left the swamp.

B. Scanning for Details

Scan the paragraphs for details. It is not necessary to read the whole passage again. Some of the following sentences have incorrect facts. Cross out the incorrect fact and write the correct answer above it.

1. The swampers were originally a small group of Georgia pioneers.

2. Swampers didn't have books and newspapers, so they wrote their own.

3. The name Okefenokee is from a French word that means "dark and mysterious."

4. The Okefenokee Swamp covers 660 square miles and is located in southeastern Georgia.

5. The swampers lived a very advanced way of life and often had contact with the outside world.

6. The swampers developed their own way of speaking and also had a way of communicating called "hollerin'."

7. Today, the Okefenokee Swamp is a national park.

8. The swamp is dark and misty, with thick forests and many plant-filled lakes.

9. The swampers lived difficult and harsh lives in the swamp.

10. When the state transferred the swamp to the federal government, all the wild animals were still living there.

C. Order of Events

Number the sentences to show the correct order.

_____ Hundreds of trees were cut down.

_____ The swampers built houses and planted gardens.

_____ The federal government created a wildlife preserve.

_____ The Native Americans used the swamp as a hiding place.

_____ A lumber company laid railroad tracks across the swamp.

_____ A group of Georgia pioneers moved into the swamp.

_____ The lumber company town was abandoned.

D. Making Inferences and Drawing Conclusions

The answers to these questions are not directly stated in the passage. Circle the letter of the best answer.

1. From the passage, it can be concluded that
   a. the swamp completely recovered from the lumber company's work there.
   b. the cutting down of the swamp's biggest trees was harmful to the animal life there.
   c. the swampers were happy to see the lumber company move in.

2. It can be inferred from the passage that
   a. many people had explored the swamp before 1850 and wanted to live there.
   b. it was impossible to live in the swamp without bringing in food from the outside.
   c. before the swampers came, few people besides the natives had gone into the swamp.

3. The passage implies that
   a. the swampers were a resourceful people who enjoyed their lives away from the rest of the world.
   b. most of the swampers really wanted to live in towns.
   c. the swampers were a backward, uncreative people who didn't know how to communicate with others.

DISCUSSION

Discuss the answers to these questions with your classmates.

1. Would you like to live in a swamp? Why or why not?

2. Why do you think that people who live in isolated places develop their own customs and ways of talking?

3. Would you like to live someplace where you were completely dependent upon nature for survival? Give your reasons.

4. All countries have folk songs. What kind of subjects do people sing about in folk songs? Give an example of a folk song from your country.

WRITING

Composition: Many of the world's forests are being cut down for land and wood. Some people believe this is necessary. Others do not. State which point of view you agree with. Give reasons to support your opinion.

RESEARCH

Below is a list of six national parks. For each one, find out in what state it is located and what its outstanding features are.

1. Denali   3. Grand Canyon   5. Sequoia

2. Everglades   4. Isle Royale   6. Yellowstone

for shipping between Great Lakes ports and **host** to more than 250,000 pleasure boats. It is a place where the past and the future meet, a city of skyscrapers and historic buildings. Most importantly, it is a place where people live and work and dream.

VOCABULARY

What is the meaning of the underlined words? Circle the letter of the correct answer. Use a dictionary to check your answers.

1. Detroit was <u>claimed</u> by the French in 1634.

   a. destroyed completely

   b. taken over as rightful owner

   c. left behind

2. The French built their first <u>mission</u> in Detroit.

   a. village

   b. place where people of a religious group work and live

   c. building to house soldiers

3. The Indians lived peacefully <u>alongside</u> the fur-trading centers.

   a. together with

   b. close to

   c. behind

4. The French lost their American <u>territories</u>.

   a. trade

   b. friends

   c. areas of land

5. The Native Americans <u>seized</u> one fort after another.

   a. captured

   b. burned

   c. built

6. Ford could not get his automobile out of his work <u>shed</u>.

   a. a building where cars are kept

   b. a small building where things are stored

   c. a building where goods are manufactured

7. Cars <u>sold like hotcakes</u>.

   a. sold very rapidly

   b. sold at a lower price

   c. sold regularly

8. Detroit has a <u>thriving</u> music industry.

   a. particular

   b. successful

   c. exciting

9. Detroit has a <u>diverse</u> population.

   a. varied

   b. separate

   c. unusual

10. Detroit is <u>host</u> to more than 250,000 pleasure boats.

    a. a provider of facilities

    b. the entrance

    c. the builder for

COMPREHENSION

A. Skimming for Main Ideas

Circle the letter of the best answer.

1. The main topic of Paragraph 4 is
   - **a.** Henry Ford was proud of his invention.
   - **b.** the first cars were produced in Detroit in 1896.
   - **c.** Henry Ford had made a car that was too big for his shed.

2. Paragraph 5 discusses how
   - **a.** Detroit became the country's top car manufacturing city.
   - **b.** the streets of Detroit have unusual names.
   - **c.** Olds and Buick started car companies in Detroit.

3. Paragraph 6 is mainly about
   - **a.** the first immigrants to come to Detroit.
   - **b.** the special traditions in Detroit.
   - **c.** the different ethnic groups found in Detroit.

4. The main topic of the last paragraph is
   - **a.** Detroit is a city of culture.
   - **b.** Detroit is more than just a car town.
   - **c.** Detroit is a modern city too.

B. Scanning for Details

Scan the paragraphs for details. It is not necessary to read the whole passage again. Circle T if the statement is true. Circle F if the statement is false.

1. Detroit attracted immigrants because it was a beautiful, modern city. **T F**
2. One of the largest and earliest groups to go to Detroit were the Greeks. **T F**
3. The name Detroit comes from a French word meaning "strait." **T F**
4. Chief Pontiac and the Ottawa people fought the French fur traders. **T F**
5. Detroit has a large population of African-Americans. **T F**
6. Detroit's location on the Detroit River makes it a center for shipping. **T F**
7. Detroit is better known for its riverfront festivals than its car manufacturing. **T F**

8. Detroit has yearly festivals celebrating its ethnic diversity. **T F**

9. Detroit is the capital of Michigan. **T F**

10. Charles King was the first person to produce a car in Detroit. **T F**

C. Order of Events

Number the sentences to show the correct order.

_____ Michigan was claimed by the French.

_____ The Olds Motor Works was founded.

_____ Native American tribes inhabited Michigan.

_____ Motown music was created.

_____ Antoine de la Mothe Cadillac established a fur-trading center called Detroit.

_____ African-Americans moved from the South to go to work in Detroit.

_____ Michigan became America's 26th state.

D. Making Inferences and Drawing Conclusions

The answers to these questions are not directly stated in the passage. Circle the letter of the best answer.

1. From the passage, it can be concluded that

    a. Henry Ford is completely responsible for making Detroit what it is today.

    b. car manufacturing was the foundation upon which Detroit was built.

    c. only recently has Detroit been an ethnically diverse city.

2. It can be inferred from the passage that

    a. Detroit grew very slowly over the years.

    b. some cars got their names from Michigan's historical people.

    c. immigration has not had much effect on cultural activities in Detroit.

3. The passage implies that

    a. modern Detroit is not as dependent upon the automobile industry as it once was.

    b. African-Americans went to work in Detroit even though life in the South was more pleasant.

    c. most of the ethnic groups of Detroit are ancestors of the first immigrants who moved there in the early 1900s.

DISCUSSION

Discuss the answers to these questions with your classmates.

1. Would you like to live in a big city or in the country? Give your reasons.
2. Compare American cars with foreign cars. What kind of car would you like to buy?
3. What do you think cars will be like 20 years from now?
4. Describe what you think life will be like in a city of the future.

WRITING

Composition: Describe three ways in which immigrants influence the culture in a city.

RESEARCH

Find the following facts about Michigan.

1. Population
2. Number of lakes
3. Area in square miles
4. State flower

5. What Battle Creek is famous for
6. What Mackinac Bridge is known for
7. What president came from Michigan

LIVING THINGS

Part 3

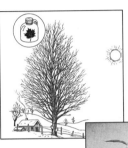

Unit 12
Maples and Pecans

Unit 13
The Turkey

Unit 14
The All-Important Pumpkin

Unit 15
The Spirit of the Wolf

MAPLES AND PECANS

What is your favorite tree?

Look at the picture. Why do you think there is a container attached to the tree?

What kind of nut trees do you have in your country?

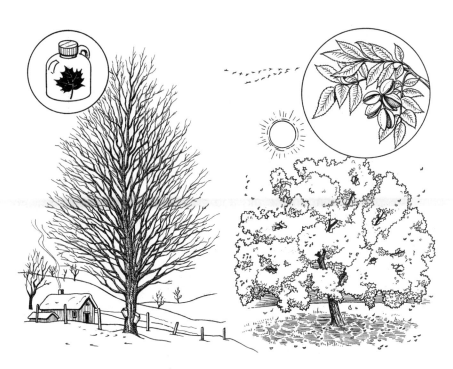

1   Today's national forests are interesting places to camp, hike, and take pictures. But for the Native Americans and early settlers, forests provided their major food sources. In the woods, they hunted animals, fished in lakes and streams, and gathered nuts and berries. They even found a source of sugar. Two trees of great importance to both the natives and settlers were the maple in the northeast and the pecan in the central south.

2   The sugar maple tree is a tall tree, reaching a height of 75 to 100 feet. It is found in the eastern half of North America. But it is most **abundant** in the forests of New England and southeastern Canada. Its hard wood is often used for furniture and flooring. Its leaves turn red, gold, and orange in the autumn.

3   During the summer, the leaves absorb energy from the sun. It is used to manufacture sugar, or glucose. From glucose, the tree creates starch, which

it stores in its roots and **trunk**. During the winter, the starch is changed into another sugar, sucrose. It mixes with water to create sap, which flows through the tree in early spring to nourish it as it begins its new growth. The sugar maple has many gallons of sap flowing through it at the end of winter when the days are warm but the nights are still cold.

4   No one knows how the Native Americans discovered the sweet, watery maple sap. But they had many uses for it and stored it in containers they called *mokuks*. When the sap began to flow, or "run," they cut a hole in the bark. Then they put in a wood **chip** to guide the sap into the *mokuk*. This is called "tapping." Native families camped in the maple **grove** until the sap stopped running in the early spring. It was one of their most important foods. A supply of maple sugar saved them from starvation when hunters returned empty-handed. They used it on everything, including meat and fish. They mixed it with corn and wheat to make cakes and a thick soup. They boiled it to make a syrup. Most often they boiled it until it was almost dry, so it could be easily stored.

5   The Native Americans gave the settlers their first taste of maple sugar. That was all they needed. Soon it became an important food for them, just as it was for the natives. For many New England settlers, it was their only source of sugar. When the words, "Sap's running!" were heard, the men quickly gathered their equipment and brought it to the groves. They made holes in the trees and put in wooden **spouts** to guide the sap into their wooden containers. As the containers filled, they carried them to the campsite where they boiled the sap. It was **tedious** work, but an exciting time too. There was a feeling of spring in the air, and everywhere the **aroma** of sweet maple syrup.

6   Maple sugar was a common, everyday sweetener in country kitchens. Today, maple syrup and sugar are luxury products. It takes 25 to 30 gallons of sap to produce one gallon of syrup. Most candy, ice cream, and pancake syrups have artificial maple flavoring. Maple syrup has become a rare treat, except for those lucky enough to live in a maple grove, of course.

7   While northerners have their maples, southerners have their pecan trees. Pecans are important for their nuts. The central southern area of the United States is the only area of the world where the pecan tree grows wild. Native pecan trees grow in greatest numbers in Texas, Oklahoma, Arkansas, Louisiana, and Mississippi. **Cultivated** pecan trees also produce crops in Georgia, Alabama, New Mexico, North and South Carolina, and Florida.

8   The pecan has an average height of 75 feet, although some wild trees have grown as tall as 160 feet. The pecan nuts grow in **clusters** and have reddish-brown shells. The pecan gets its name from the Native American word *pacanes*, a word the natives used for all nuts with hard shells. The pecan was an important food source for both the natives and settlers. The meat of the nut is rich and **nourishing**. It was the custom for natives and settlers to go nutting every autumn. People gathered wild nuts and stored them for winter use.

9   Although there are still some wild nut trees, most of our nuts are grown in groves. Nut trees grow slowly. A few nuts develop on most cultivated trees by age three or four. The pounds of nuts harvested increase with the age of

the tree. A 15- to 20-year-old tree produces 75 to 100 pounds. Pecan trees continue producing nuts when they are over 100 years old. One pecan tree in Texas has set a record for producing 1,000 pounds of pecans in one season. That would make quite a pecan pie!

VOCABULARY

Complete each definition with one of the following words. Guess your answers, then check with a dictionary.

abundant	trunk	grove	nourishing
chip	spouts	tedious	
aroma	clusters	cultivated	

1. A small piece of wood or other material broken off from something is a
   _____ .

2. If something is plentiful, it is _____ .

3. The main thick stem of a tree is its _____ .

4. The _____ is the characteristic, pleasant smell of something.

5. Work that is _____ is tiring because it is long and boring.

6. When a number of things of the same kind grow in groups, they grow in
   _____ .

7. The place in which a group of fruit or nut trees grows is a _____ .

8. If something is _____ , it gives food value to your body and is nutritious.

9. Trees that are _____ are grown as crops from seeds.

10. _____ are openings from which liquid comes out, as a small tube or pipe.

COMPREHENSION

A. Skimming for Main Ideas

Circle the letter of the best answer.

1. Paragraph 2 is mainly about
   a. the forests of New England and southeastern Canada.
   b. the characteristics of the sugar maple.
   c. the height of the sugar maple.

2. The main topic of Paragraph 3 is
   a. what happens to the sugar maple in the summer.
   b. how the sugar maple makes its sugary sap.
   c. why the sugar maple has sugar in the winter.

3. The main topic of Paragraph 5 is
   a. the importance of maple sugar to the settlers.
   b. the difficulty of making maple syrup.
   c. the equipment needed to extract sap from trees.

4. The last paragraph is mainly about
   a. the amount of nuts older pecan trees produce and how they are used in pies.
   b. the characteristics of the growth and production of nut trees.
   c. the advanced age of some pecan trees.

B. Scanning for Details

Find the details to complete these sentences as quickly as possible. It is not necessary to read the whole passage again.

1. The Native Americans collected the maple sugar sap in containers called
   _____ .

2. For many New England settlers, the maple sap was their only source of
   _____ .

3. The sugar maple tree reaches a height of _____ .

4. The pecan tree was an important food source for both the natives and settlers
   because _____ .

5. The only area of the world where pecan trees grow wild is _____

_____ .

6. The sap flows in the maple at the end of winter when _____

_____ .

7. Making a hole in the maple tree and putting in a piece of wood to guide the flow of the

sap is called _____ .

8. In order to make maple syrup, the sap must be _____ .

9. A 20-year-old pecan tree produces _____ pounds of pecans in a season.

10. Today, real maple syrup is a luxury item because it takes _____ gallons
of sap to make one gallon of syrup.

C. Order of Events

Number the sentences to show the correct order.

_____ Sap is boiled to make syrup.

_____ A hole is made in the tree and a spout put in.

_____ Maple leaves absorb energy from the sun.

_____ The sap flows through the tree to nourish its new growth.

_____ The tree changes starch to sucrose.

_____ Sap is collected in containers.

D. Making Inferences and Drawing Conclusions

**The answers to these questions are not directly stated in the passage. Circle the letter of
the best answer.**

1. From the passage, it can be concluded that

   a. the settlers did not have to depend upon nature for their survival.

   b. the settlers learned how to use the land's natural resources from the Native
Americans.

   c. the settlers had a different way of getting sap from the maple tree than the Native
Americans.

2. It can be inferred from the passage that

   a. the yearly gathering of maple sap was a difficult but rewarding task for the New England settlers.

   b. the New England settlers gathered the maple syrup for pleasure and not out of necessity.

   c. the maple sap was not as important to the Native Americans as it was to the settlers.

3. The passage implies that

   a. wild pecan trees produce more nuts than cultivated trees.

   b. pecan trees have a long and productive life.

   c. cultivated trees must be cut down every few years to make room for planting younger trees.

DISCUSSION

Discuss the answers to these questions with your classmates.

1. There are many stories about how the Native Americans may have discovered the maple sap. How do you think they discovered it?

2. How important do you think trees are to making a city or town beautiful?

3. If you had a backyard, what type of trees would you put in it? Discuss your reasons.

4. Some trees are known for their beauty. Others for their usefulness. Name some in each category.

WRITING

Composition: What is the most popular plant in your country? Describe in detail ways in which it is used.

RESEARCH

Find out what products are produced from the following trees.

1. Eucalyptus   **3.** Baobab   **5.** Jute

2. Palm   **4.** Live oak   **6.** Pine

THE TURKEY

Unit 13

What do you know about the turkey?

Do you like to eat turkey?

When do you think people eat turkey?

Wild turkey, painting by John James Audubon.

1   Can you imagine a turkey instead of an eagle on a dollar bill, at the top of a flag pole, and on the presidential seal? That's exactly what the popular Early American statesman Benjamin Franklin had in mind when he declared that the turkey should be made the symbol of the USA. That may seem **absurd** today when all we see are supermarket turkeys that end up roasted on our Thanksgiving dinner tables. But the wild turkey of Ben Franklin's day was a truly American bird that played a big part in the history of the New World.

2   Wild turkeys once inhabited territory all across North America. Before North America was settled, the Native Americans hunted turkeys for food. They also used their feathers for warm winter clothing, and their bones to

make tools and weapons. When the European settlers arrived, turkeys became their main source of food.

3　　People think turkeys are very dumb because they don't know enough to come in out of the rain. As a matter of fact, they've been known to hold their mouths open during rainstorms and drown! But that's only true of the **domesticated** turkey. The wild turkey is one of nature's most **cunning** creatures. It is a powerful and intelligent bird with beautiful, multicolored brown feathers that shine in the sunlight. Turkeys can stand four feet tall. The males, also called *toms* or *gobblers*, average over 16 pounds. The females, or hens, are over nine pounds. The wild turkey is slim compared with the meaty, domesticated bird, and its neck and legs are longer. Only when toms are **courting** do they look like the fat turkey that children draw at Thanksgiving. When they spread their tail feathers and puff up the feathers on their bodies, they look like fat, round birds rather than slim, **streamlined** ones.

4　　Wild turkeys are very **wary**, especially mothers with chicks. They are rarely seen by humans. They hide in the bushes where their natural coloring makes them just about invisible. Unlike the domesticated turkey, the wild bird is a powerful flyer. When it is frightened, the wild turkey spreads its five- to six-foot wings and flies away at up to 50 miles per hour. Even on the ground the bird is speedy and can run as fast as 25 miles per hour.

5　　These **traits** may have saved wild turkeys from their natural enemies but they were no match for the European colonists who hunted them nearly to extinction. In the early 1900s people realized that something had to be done to save the wild bird. Therefore, laws were put into effect to limit hunting, and preserves were created. Today there are over one million wild turkeys living in 42 states.

6　　Meanwhile, a domesticated variety has been **bred** by turkey farmers over the years. The result is a **tame** bird that is very different from its wild cousin, although no less important. The domesticated turkey could never live in the wild because it has lost its ability to survive in nature. It can only live in cages. The mostly white bird cannot fly because it's too heavy and is so tame that it goes immediately to humans. Like its wild cousin, however, it serves the very important purpose of feeding Americans, who **consume** almost 600 million pounds of turkey on Thanksgiving Day alone. And since nutritionists have proved that turkey is very healthy, it has become as common on the modern daily table as it was for the first settlers.

VOCABULARY

What is the meaning of the underlined words? Circle the letter of the correct answer. Use a dictionary to check your answers.

1. It seems <u>absurd</u> to have the turkey as the symbol of the USA.

   a. ideal

   b. ridiculous

   c. offensive

2. The <u>domesticated</u> turkey is known to open its mouth during a rainstorm and drown.

   a. trained to live with people and serve them

   b. living in North America

   c. female animal

3. The wild turkey is one of nature's most <u>cunning</u> creatures.

   a. fierce

   b. courageous

   c. clever

4. Tom turkeys look fat when they are <u>courting</u>.

   a. attracting the attention of females for mating

   b. getting ready to fight with other turkeys

   c. frightened by people

5. When turkeys puff up their feathers they do not look slim and <u>streamlined</u>.

   a. pear-shaped

   b. smooth and compact

   c. long and twisted

6. Wild turkeys are <u>wary</u> and are rarely seen by humans.

   a. cautious

   b. aggressive

   c. restless

7. The <u>traits</u> of the wild turkey save it from its natural enemies.

   a. characteristics

   b. tricks

   c. wisdom

8. A domesticated variety of turkey has been <u>bred</u> by farmers.

   a. improved

   b. put in cages

   c. made to produce young

9. The domesticated turkey is a <u>tame</u> bird.

   a. well-known

   b. harmless

   c. unusual

10. Americans <u>consume</u> almost 600 million pounds of turkey on Thanksgiving Day.

    a. waste

    b. freeze

    c. eat

COMPREHENSION

A. Skimming for Main Ideas

Circle the letter of the best answer.

1. Paragraph 1 is mainly about

    a. the turkey as a truly American bird.

    b. Ben Franklin's strange ideas.

    c. the supermarket turkeys we roast on Thanksgiving Day.

2. The main topic of Paragraph 4 is

    a. the speed of the wild turkey.

    b. the characteristics of the wild turkey.

    c. the size of the wild turkey.

3. The main topic of Paragraph 5 is

    a. limiting hunting of the wild turkey.

    b. European colonists hunting the wild turkey.

    c. saving the wild turkey.

4. The last paragraph is mainly about

    a. the health value of eating turkey meat.

    b. the characteristics and importance of the domesticated turkey.

    c. the amount of turkey meat consumed by Americans.

B. Scanning for Details

Scan the paragraphs for details. It is not necessary to read the whole passage again. Circle T if the statement is true. Circle F if the statement is false.

1. The domesticated turkey does not have the ability to survive in the wild. T F

2. Wild turkeys have the ability to fly, while domesticated turkeys do not. T F

3. Benjamin Franklin was thinking of domesticated turkeys when he said they should be America's symbol. T F

4. Wild turkeys are all one color while domesticated turkeys have many colors. T F

5. Many wild turkeys have been known to drown during rainstorms. T F

6. When the European settlers arrived, wild turkeys lived in most areas of North America. T F

7. In the 1700s people started protecting the turkey and putting them in preserves. T F

8. A wild turkey has more meat than a domesticated turkey. T F

9. Turkey meat is a popular food in America today. T F

10. The female wild turkey is larger than the male. T F

C. Order of Events

Number the sentences to show the correct order.

_____ Native Americans hunt wild turkeys for food.

_____ Preserves are created to try to save the wild turkey.

_____ Americans buy turkeys in modern supermarkets.

_____ European colonists hunt so many wild turkeys that they almost disappear from America.

_____ Benjamin Franklin says the turkey should be made a symbol.

D. Making Inferences and Drawing Conclusions

The answers to these questions are not directly stated in the passage. Circle the letter of the best answer.

1. From the passage, it can be concluded that
   a. the turkey has been an important food source for hundreds of years.
   b. people have not been successful in protecting the wild turkey from extinction.
   c. wild turkeys can easily be seen and caught in their natural environment.

2. It can be inferred from the passage that
   a. Benjamin Franklin should not have been a statesman.
   b. the European colonists didn't like to eat turkey.
   c. the Native Americans had many uses for the turkey.

3. The passage implies that
   a. wild turkeys have very different characteristics from domesticated turkeys.
   b. wild turkeys don't have any way to escape from their natural enemies.
   c. the wild turkey is a slow, awkward bird.

DISCUSSION

Discuss the answers to these questions with your classmates.

1. What is the most popular holiday food in your country?
2. Do you think animals should be given substances to make them grow bigger for market?
3. What animals are considered stupid? What animals are considered intelligent?
4. Do you think it is cruel to raise cattle and poultry in crowded indoor cages?

WRITING

Composition: Do you think humans should eat meat or should they be vegetarians? Give two reasons for your argument.

RESEARCH

Look up the answers to the following questions.

1. Which birds do not fly? Name three.

2. Which birds besides the turkey are eaten? Name five.

3. Which birds live by the seashore? Name five.

4. Which birds have feathers that are useful to humans? Name two.

5. What is the smallest bird and the biggest bird in North America?

THE ALL-IMPORTANT PUMPKIN

Do you like to eat pumpkin?

Do you have pumpkins in your country?

What kinds of foods can you make with pumpkin?

1   For Americans, the simple pumpkin has come to symbolize everything that is important and meaningful about autumn. Everyone knows it's autumn when pumpkins begin to appear at roadside **stands**. Soon afterward, pumpkins will decorate doorsteps at Halloween. Then they'll be part of Thanksgiving holiday decorations. They'll also be baked into breads and pies. Farmers will know winter is near when morning frost is on the pumpkin.

2   Pumpkin and squash are believed to be the first food plants cultivated by the Native Americans. New England natives called them both *askootasquash*. The Pilgrims, who were the first English settlers, shortened it to *squash*. Then they named the pumpkin from a Greek word, *pepon*, meaning a large melon. The natives cooked pumpkins in **stews** and fed uncooked pieces to their horses. They planted pumpkins among their corn. The natives taught the settlers how to plant it and eat it. Very quickly the pumpkin became a favorite and important garden vegetable. It was a healthy addition to the settlers' diets because it is rich in vitamins and minerals.

3   Eighteenth-century Americans used pumpkin seed tea for medicinal purposes. But of all the uses of pumpkins, none is as amusing as the way it was used by New Englanders, or "Yankees." Yankee men used the pumpkin **shell** as a guide for cutting their hair! They put the pumpkin on their head and **trimmed** around its base. This gave rise to the expression "pumpkinhead,"

which at first meant New Englander, and later meant someone who looked silly or stupid.

4   Every autumn there are pumpkin festivals held all over the country. They are a type of **harvest** celebration. Pumpkin queens and kings are named. Prizes are given for the biggest or the best-decorated pumpkin, or the best-tasting pumpkin pie. With the help of fertilizers, some pumpkins have been grown to the size of a small car.

5   Pumpkins are popular with children, not so much for eating as for making jack-o'-lanterns at Halloween. Most Americans don't realize that this tradition comes all the way from Ireland and Scotland. It originated over 2,000 years ago with the Celts who lived in what is now France and the British Isles. They celebrated a harvest festival on October 31. It was a joyous occasion, but also in some ways a sad one. It marked the beginning of the long, dark, cold winter. They believed that in the darkness, the spirits of the dead walked upon the earth. Great fires were built on the hills to protect the people from bad spirits. People **hollowed out** turnips, a root plant, and put a candle inside. They carried them if they went outside to protect themselves from evil spirits.

6   When the settlers came to America, they brought their customs with them. They didn't have turnips, so they used pumpkins instead. Today, of course, children look forward to Halloween and the carving of pumpkins. First the pumpkin is hollowed out and the seeds and **pulp** taken out. Then funny or scary faces are carved into the side. In the evening, a candle is put inside and the face **glows** in the dark. Sometimes pumpkins are painted and decorated. As Halloween approaches, jack-o'-lanterns **pop up** on doorsteps everywhere.

7   After Halloween, Americans look forward to the Thanksgiving holiday. Pumpkins and corn plants are often used as decorations during this time. They symbolize autumn and the spirit of the season. It is a time of giving thanks for the harvest, for the family, and for all the good things that families enjoy.

8   But pumpkins don't only serve as symbols. They're eaten too. The first settlers who depended on the pumpkin for food would be amazed to see how many ways it's eaten today. Pumpkins are boiled, **broiled**, and baked. They're put in bread, cakes, pies, muffins, doughnuts, ice cream, pancakes, cookies, soups, and even hamburgers! Sometimes there seems to be no end to the uses of pumpkins. Who would ever have thought this simple little plant would get to be so popular!

VOCABULARY

What is the meaning of the underlined words? Circle the letter of the correct answer. Use a dictionary to check your answers.

1. In autumn, pumpkins begin to appear at roadside <u>stands</u>.

   a. stations

   b. small outdoor stores

   c. storage areas

2. The Native Americans cooked pumpkins in a <u>stew</u>.

   a. a meal of meat and vegetables cooked in a liquid.

   b. a dessert made with sweet fruit and vegetables

   c. a kind of flat bread

3. The pumpkin <u>shell</u> was used as a guide for cutting hair by the Yankee men.

   a. the hard upper end

   b. the soft and watery inside seed

   c. the hard outside covering

4. They <u>trimmed</u> their hair around the pumpkin's base.

   a. cut

   b. decorated

   c. curled

5. Pumpkin festivals are a kind of <u>harvest</u> celebration.

   a. crop planting

   b. crop gathering

   c. crop growing

6. People <u>hollowed out</u> turnips and put a candle inside.

   a. cut into and emptied the inside of

   b. made a small hole in

   c. put in the oven and dried out

7. The seeds and <u>pulp</u> of the pumpkin are taken out.

   a. the thick skin

   b. the sweet juice

   c. the soft inside part

8. The face on the pumpkin <u>glows</u> in the dark.

   a. looks as if it is moving with light

   b. gives out a warm light

   c. sends out flashes of light

9. Jack-o'-lanterns <u>pop up</u> on doorsteps as Halloween approaches.

   a. appear

   b. shine

   c. become ripe

10. Pumpkins are boiled, <u>broiled</u>, and baked.

    a. fried in hot oil

    b. grilled under or over a flame

    c. heated in an oven

COMPREHENSION

A. Skimming for Main Ideas

Circle the letter of the best answer.

1. The main topic of Paragraph 2 is

    a. the value of the pumpkin as a nutritious food.

    b. how the pumpkin got its name.

    c. the history of the pumpkin in Early America.

2. The main topic of Paragraph 3 is

    a. the use of the pumpkin by 18th-century Americans.

    b. the use of the pumpkin for cutting hair.

    c. the use of the pumpkin in medicine.

3. Paragraph 4 is mainly about

    a. the size of pumpkins.

    b. pumpkin festivals around the country.

    c. choosing a pumpkin queen and king.

4. The last paragraph is mainly about

    a. the popularity of the pumpkin as food.

    b. the use of the pumpkin as a symbol.

    c. pumpkins eaten in desserts.

B. Scanning for Details

Find the details as quickly as possible and circle the letter of the correct answer. It is not necessary to read the whole passage again.

1. Eighteenth-century Americans used pumpkin seeds to make

    a. puddings.

    b. medicinal tea.

    c. candles.

2. At Halloween, pumpkins

    a. decorate doorsteps.

    b. are used to cut hair.

    c. are carried for protection.

3. When frost appears on the pumpkin, farmers know

    a. it's time to harvest their crops.

    b. winter is near.

    c. they have to plow their fields.

4. The early settlers depended on the pumpkin for

    a. food.

    b. clothing.

    c. decoration.

5. The Native Americans taught the settlers how to

    a. carve pumpkins.

    b. cut their hair using pumpkin shells.

    c. plant and eat pumpkins.

6. For Americans, the pumpkin is not only a food, but also a

    a. toy.

    b. form of protection.

    c. symbol.

7. The tradition of carving jack-o'-lanterns comes from

   a. Irish and Scottish immigrants.

   b. the Native Americans.

   c. American farmers.

8. To carve a pumpkin, the first step is to

   a. take out the seeds and pulp.

   b. put in a candle.

   c. paint and decorate it.

9. Today, pumpkins

   a. are no longer popular.

   b. have many uses.

   c. are smaller than they used to be.

10. The Native Americans used to plant pumpkins

   a. on hills.

   b. in the winter.

   c. with their corn.

C. Order of Events

Number the sentences to show the correct order.

_____ The Native Americans taught the settlers how to grow pumpkins.

_____ The Celts hollowed out turnips and put candles inside.

_____ Pumpkins are used in everything from doughnuts to ice cream.

_____ The pumpkin became an important garden vegetable for the settlers.

D. Making Inferences and Drawing Conclusions

The answers to these questions are not directly stated in the passage. Circle the letter of the best answer.

1. From the passage, it can be concluded that

   a. today, the pumpkin is more useful as a decoration than as a food source.

   b. children eat pumpkin more often than adults eat it.

   c. the pumpkin is as useful and important today as it was 200 years ago.

2. It can be inferred from the passage that

   a. the Native Americans helped the settlers survive in the New World.

   b. the Native Americans didn't know much about farming.

   c. the European settlers didn't have much use for the pumpkin.

3. The passage implies that

   a. pumpkins were not important to the Native Americans.

   b. it wasn't easy to grow pumpkins in America.

   c. the settlers had never seen pumpkins before they came to America.

DISCUSSION

Discuss the answers to these questions with your classmates.

1. What vegetable or fruit has a special meaning in your country? Explain what it symbolizes.

2. What vegetable or fruit in your country has many uses? Describe the different uses.

3. Explain what special fruits or vegetables are eaten during holidays in your country.

4. Do you have harvest celebrations in your country? Describe what takes place.

WRITING

Composition: What is the most important food in your country? State two reasons why it is important and give examples of how it can be prepared.

RESEARCH

Find out what fruit or vegetable the following states are known for.

1. Idaho
2. Iowa
3. Washington
4. Massachusetts
5. Florida
6. Hawaii
7. Minnesota

THE SPIRIT OF THE WOLF

What do you know about the wolf?

Do you have wolves in your country?

What stories do you know that involve the wolf?

1 The Native Americans had great respect for nature and all its creatures. They depended upon animals for food, clothing, and shelter. They also admired animals for their cunning, strength, and **agility**. Newborn babies were often named after an animal, such as Running Deer or Little Eagle. An important chief of the Cheyenne people was named High Backed Wolf. To Native Americans, the wolf was a very special animal.

2 The Native Americans believed that the world was filled with spirits that controlled their lives. All things in nature, such as the sun, the mountains, the snake, eagle, and wolf had a spirit within it. To **honor** the spirits and ask them for help, ceremonies were performed. One of them was the animal dance of

the Cheyenne. For this ceremony, many special **rites** were performed. One was the painting of a wolfskin in a certain manner. Another was when the men put on skins of various animals, including the wolf. They danced around a special fire. It was believed this ceremony would bring the tribe good fortune when they went out to hunt. It was important to have the spirit of the wolf with them. The natives knew the wolf was a great hunter. They also admired its many other qualities.

3   In the wild, wolves have great strength and **endurance**. Their thick fur protects them from temperatures as low as 50 degrees below zero. They travel in family groups called *packs* and are intelligent, loving, and **loyal**. There are a number of wolf species. In America, the Arctic wolf and the timber wolf are found, as well as the smaller and darker red wolf of Texas, and the Mexican wolf. Wolves can adapt to a variety of habitats.

4   The northern wolf is a very handsome animal that looks like a big, friendly dog. In the far north, it is often white. In the south, it is gray. Wolves are very social animals. They travel, hunt, and perform almost all other activities in the company of other wolves. A pack usually consists of a male and female that will stay together for life and have babies, or pups. They are constant and loving companions. The other members are usually their young, ranging in age from tiny pups to two- and three-year-olds. Most packs include six or seven members but have been known to include as many as 15.

5   The parent wolves are the leaders. The rest of the wolves, depending upon their age and strength, all have their own special places. Their relationships are very complicated. Scientific studies have shown that wolf packs have **complex** rules that govern their behavior and the way they relate to each other. Their methods of communicating are also very elaborate. Although wolves make many different kinds of sounds, the most famous is the **howl**. Wolves howl at any time, not just at night. It's a way of sharing their closeness as a group. One wolf will point its nose toward the sky and start to howl. Immediately the other pack members will rush over and join him. The whole group is excited and happy. Packs also communicate with each other this way. They tell each other to stay out of their territory.

6   In wolf families, everything is done as a group, including the raising of the young. They trust and depend on each other from birth. Probably the most important activity in the life of the pack is hunting. Wolves are carnivorous, or meat eaters. They live on a variety of foods, from mice to fish to the larger deer and moose. Wolves only kill what they can eat. Hunting in packs is necessary for chasing and killing large prey. Wolves never attack a large, healthy deer or moose, which can easily defend itself with sharp kicks. Wolves **pursue** herds to find the sick or weak members. This may seem cruel, but they are actually doing the herd good by keeping it strong. Also, without natural enemies, herds will overpopulate their territory and use up the food supply. Many will eventually starve. Wolves are needed to keep the balance of nature.

7   Unfortunately, the people who settled America did not respect the wolf like the natives did. Over the years, wolves were hunted, poisoned, and destroyed in great numbers. They are now rare in North America. However, many people now believe the wolf has a rightful place among America's

wildlife. In some places, like Yellowstone National Park, they have been put back into the wild. There is much **controversy** about this. Ranchers believe the wolves will attack their herds. Hunters also don't like wolves in the wild. They want the deer to overpopulate so they can hunt them. At the same time, there are many people who are fighting to let the wolf once again **roam** freely in the remaining wild lands of America. The argument over putting wolves back into the wild is certain to continue for many years. Only time will tell whether they will one day be allowed to do that, and if the spirit of the wolf will live on.

VOCABULARY

What is the meaning of the underlined words? Circle the letter of the correct answer. Use a dictionary to check your answers.

1. Animals are admired for their cunning, strength, and <u>agility</u>.

   a. gentleness

   b. quickness

   c. cautiousness

2. The Native Americans performed ceremonies to <u>honor</u> the spirits.

   a. show respect

   b. accept

   c. ask favors from

3. For the ceremony, they performed special <u>rites</u>.

   a. rhythmic movements

   b. religious celebrations

   c. fixed ceremonial actions

4. Wolves have great strength and <u>endurance</u>.

   a. tolerance for hardship

   b. vitality

   c. dependability

5. Wolves are intelligent, loving, and <u>loyal</u>.

   a. courageous

   b. faithful

   c. obedient

6. Wolves have <u>complex</u> rules that govern their behavior.

   a. complicated

   b. simple

   c. strange

7. Wolves are famous for their <u>howl</u>.

   a. short, sharp sound

   b. long, loud cry

   c. low, continuous sound

8. Wolves <u>pursue</u> herds of deer.

   a. watch

   b. discover

   c. chase

9. There is much <u>controversy</u> about putting wolves <u>back</u> into the wild.

    a. talk

    b. rumor

    c. argument

10. Many people want to let the wolf <u>roam</u> freely in the wild.

    a. wander about

    b. struggle along

    c. run quickly

COMPREHENSION

A. Skimming for Main Ideas

Circle the letter of the best answer.

1. Paragraph 2 is mainly about

    a. what the Native Americans believed in.

    b. why the Cheyenne performed the animal dance.

    c. when the Native Americans performed ceremonies.

2. The main topic of Paragraph 4 is

    a. the characteristics and habits of the wolf.

    b. how the wolf survives as a social animal.

    c. the relationship between male and female wolves.

3. The main topic of Paragraph 6 is

    a. how wolves depend on each other.

    b. the hunting activity of a wolf pack.

    c. what wolves like to eat.

4. The last paragraph is mainly about

    a. why people killed the wolf.

    b. the life of the wolf in Yellowstone National Park.

    c. the debate over putting wolves back into the wild.

B. Scanning for Details

Scan the paragraphs for details. It is not necessary to read the whole passage again. Some of the following sentences have incorrect facts. Cross out the incorrect fact and write the correct answer above it.

1. Wolves that are found in the far north are often dark red.

2. The Native Americans believed that natural things like mountains and animals had spirits in them.

3. The Native Americans admired and depended upon animals, and often gave their children animal names.

4. Wolves most often hunt alone.

5. The leaders of a wolf pack are the three-year-old wolves.

6. Wolves howl together to share their anger.

7. Wolves are intelligent, loving, and loyal animals.

8. The animal dance of the Cheyenne was done to honor the spirits and ask them for their help.

9. Wolves are needed to use up the food supply.

10. Wolves usually attack large, healthy deer.

C. Order of Events

Number the sentences to show the correct order.

_____ Wolves are put back into the wild in Yellowstone National Park.

_____ Wolves were hunted and destroyed in great numbers.

_____ The Native Americans respected animals and depended upon them for survival.

_____ European settlers came to America.

D. Making Inferences and Drawing Conclusions

The answers to these questions are not directly stated in the passage. Circle the letter of the best answer.

1. From the passage, it can be concluded that
   a. wolves are dangerous and frightening animals that should be kept in cages.
   b. wolves are not useful in modern society.
   c. wolves have characteristics that can be admired and respected by humans.

2. It can be inferred from the passage that
   a. Native Americans were close to nature and knew the characteristics and habits of animals.
   b. Native Americans hunted wolves and were fearful of them.
   c. the settlers killed wolves in large numbers because wolves were killing all the healthy deer they depended on for food.

3. The passage implies that

    a. wolves will soon be living in the wild in the large numbers they once were.

    b. it is not likely that wolves will be put back into the wild throughout the United States in the near future.

    c. wolves will probably be extinct in a few years.

DISCUSSION

Discuss the answers to these questions with your classmates.

1. Do you think the wolf should be reintroduced into the wild?

2. People are often described in animal terms, such as "brave as a lion" or "gentle as a lamb." Discuss some of the characteristics of animals and how they are reflected in people.

3. Do you think people should keep wild animals as pets? Why or why not?

4. How have humans upset the balance of nature?

WRITING

Composition: What is your favorite animal? State two reasons for your choice.

RESEARCH

Look up the animals in the list below. Find out in what regions of the United States they are found, what is their habitat (the environment in which they live), and two characteristics of the animal.

1. Otter	**4.** Bald eagle	**7.** Caribou	**10.** Moose
2. Rattlesnake	**5.** Manatee	**8.** Alligator	
3. Walrus	**6.** Roadrunner	**9.** Bighorn sheep	

GREAT MOMENTS

Part 4

A PERFECT LUNAR LANDING

Would you like to go to the moon?

Which other planet would you like to visit?

Would you like to live in a space station?

1   On July 16, 1969, after traveling 239,000 miles into space, the *Apollo 11* spacecraft slowly circled around the moon. Attached to it was the *Eagle*, a smaller spacecraft called a **lunar** module. With two astronauts aboard, it separated from the *Apollo 11*. It **drifted** downward and landed without a splash on the moon's Sea of Tranquility. Then one of the most memorable moments in American and scientific history occurred. Neil Armstrong, dressed in a white spacesuit, stepped down from his spacecraft onto the moon. He became the first human being to **set foot** on another world.

2   Neil was soon joined by Buzz Aldrin, and together they explored the moon on foot. It was a very different world from our own. On the moon there is no air, water, clouds, weather, or sound, since sound travels on air. There are no living things. The ground is **barren** and is covered with gray rock and gray, powder-like soil. The daytime temperature is hot enough to boil water at 212 degrees Fahrenheit. At night it would freeze it instantly, as it drops to about 280 degrees below zero. There is no water on the moon, however. It is drier than any desert on earth.

3   There are large dark areas on the moon, hundreds of miles across. They are made from rock inside the moon that melted, flowed out, and flooded the lowlands. An Italian astronomer named Giovanni Riccioli used a telescope to map the moon 350 years ago. He thought the smooth, dark areas were seas. Although we know better now, we still call these areas seas, like the Sea of Tranquility. That's where Aldrin and Armstrong walked, picked up samples of rock and soil, set up experiments, and took photographs. They even enjoyed themselves by taking great leaps, jumping farther than even the greatest athlete, due to the much weaker **gravity**. Overweight people would like it on the moon because you weigh six times less there than you weigh on earth. When the astronauts returned to *Apollo 11*, they left behind a plaque that said, "Here men from the planet earth first set foot upon the moon, July 1969, A.D. We came in peace for all mankind."

4   Five more landings were made on the moon over the next three and a half years. Ten more astronauts became "moon walkers." They explored various regions from the flat "seas" to the **rugged** highlands. On the last three missions, they were able to cover more territory because they had a vehicle called a lunar rover, or "moon buggy." It was **collapsible**. It was powered by electric motors and was able to carry two astronauts and their equipment at a top speed of nine miles an hour.

5   *Apollo 17* was the last spacecraft to take men to the moon in December 1972. Altogether there were six successful landings by *Apollo 11, 12, 14, 15, 16,* and *17.* Unlucky *Apollo 13* was damaged by an explosion on the way to the moon. The crew had to use their lunar module to make it safely back to earth.

6   Early in the 21st century, a moon base is expected to be built. Scientific laboratories and observatories will be built, as well as **living quarters**. There will be lunar **ferries** that will travel to the moon and back with scientists and engineers aboard. Later, interplanetary **craft** will be built to carry explorers to Mars and perhaps one day to other planets in our universe.

VOCABULARY

Complete each definition with one of the following words or phrases. Guess your answers, then check with a dictionary.

lunar	drifted	barren	craft
set foot	rugged	gravity	
ferries	living quarters	collapsible	

1. If something is _____ it can be bent or folded to make it smaller.

2. Something that is of, to, or for the moon is called _____ .

3. The place or area where people lodge or live in are _____ .

4. _____ is the natural force by which objects are attracted to each other.

5. Land that is _____ is not productive and has nothing on it.

6. To _____ is to visit or enter a place.

7. _____ take people or things across a sea or continent in an organized service or route.

8. Land that is _____ is rough and uneven.

9. A vessel or a ship that travels through the air or in the sea is a

   _____ .

10. _____ means floated or driven by currents or the wind.

COMPREHENSION

A. Skimming for Main Ideas

Circle the letter of the best answer.

1. The main topic of Paragraph 1 is
   a. how man first landed on the moon.
   b. what a lunar module is.
   c. the job of Neil Armstrong on the moon.

2. Paragraph 2 is mainly about

    a. how Neil Armstrong and Buzz Aldrin explored the moon.

    b. the temperature of the moon.

    c. the characteristics of the moon.

3. The main topic of Paragraph 4 is

    a. collapsible moon buggies.

    b. the five other landings on the moon.

    c. the astronauts who walked on the moon.

4. The last paragraph is mainly about the fact that

    a. a moon base is expected in the next century.

    b. there are plans for future space travel and living.

    c. ferries will travel to the moon from earth.

B. Scanning for Details

Find the details to complete these sentences as quickly as possible. It is not necessary to read the whole passage again.

1. An Italian astronomer by the name of _____

    used a _____ to map the moon 350 years ago.

2. On the last three moon missions, the astronauts used a _____ , or

    "_____," to travel on the surface of the moon.

3. On the first lunar landing, the *Eagle* landed on an area of the moon called

    _____ .

4. The last spacecraft to take men to the moon in December 1972 was

    _____ .

5. The surface of the moon is covered with _____

    _____ .

6. In the early part of the 21st century, Americans expect to build a

    _____ on the moon.

7. The daytime temperature on the moon is _____ , which is hot

    enough to _____ .

8. There is no sound on the moon because _____

_____ .

9. A person's weight on the moon is _____ than their
weight on earth.

10. *Apollo 13* never made it to the moon because _____

_____ .

C. Order of Events

Number the sentences to show the correct order.

_____ Buzz Aldrin and Neil Armstrong collected samples of rock and soil.

_____ *Apollo 13* made it safely back to earth.

_____ The *Eagle* module separated from *Apollo 11*.

_____ A plaque was placed on the moon.

_____ Neil Armstrong stepped onto the moon.

_____ Electric vehicles were used to explore the moon's surface.

D. Making Inferences and Drawing Conclusions

The answers to these questions are not directly stated in the passage. Circle the letter of the best answer.

1. From the passage, it can be concluded that

    a. people will go to the moon to lose weight.

    b. people could live comfortably on the moon if there was water there.

    c. living on the moon would be very different from life here on earth.

2. It can be inferred from the passage that

    a. astronomers have always been limited by the tools they have to work with.

    b. astronomers found water on the moon 350 years ago.

    c. scientists today don't make mistakes as they did in the past.

3. The passage implies that

    a. humans will never get used to traveling through space.

    b. space travel will one day be an ordinary part of life.

    c. there are no longer any dangers involving space travel.

DISCUSSION

Discuss the answers to these questions with your classmates.

1. Billions of dollars have been spent on space exploration. Do you think this is a waste of taxpayer money?

2. Science-fiction programs about space are very popular. Why do you think this is so? Name some of the programs currently on television that are about space travel and living.

3. The science of astronomy has existed for thousands of years. Why have people always been so curious about the stars and planets?

4. Astrology is the study of how the planets affect our lives. Do you believe in the astrological signs (signs of the Zodiac)?

WRITING

Composition: Describe what you think life will be like on a space station.

RESEARCH

Find out the following facts about our moon, Jupiter, Mars, and Venus.

1. Distance from the earth

2. Diameter at equator (size around the middle)

3. Size in relation to the earth

4. Average surface temperature

5. Does it have a moon or moons?

JONAS SALK DISCOVERS THE POLIO VACCINE

What are some of the major diseases in the world today?

Which diseases have cures?

Which diseases do not have cures at this time?

1   A terrible disease called polio **struck** the United States in the late 1940s and early 1950s. It **crippled** 300,000 people, mostly children, and killed 57,000. There was no cure for the disease, although scientists were working hard to find one. Finally the National Foundation for Infantile Paralysis, better known as the March of Dimes, with the contributions from millions of Americans, began a research program at the University of Pittsburgh Medical School. They asked Dr. Jonas Salk, who was already known for his work on flu viruses, to direct the program. Salk joined the fight against polio.

2   Salk knew the only way to stop the disease was to develop a vaccine, a serum containing a small amount of the killed virus. When this vaccine was injected into a person's body, it would cause the body to fight the virus and make it harmless. Once this occurred, the body would be protected against the live virus. Salk concentrated all his energy on developing the vaccine. Sometimes he worked 20 hours a day, seven days a week with his **dedicated**

staff. Finally, after much testing, Salk was so sure of his vaccine's success that he tested it on himself. Then he gave it to his wife and children. The vaccine was then tried on 500 volunteers. It proved successful every time.

3   On April 12, 1955, medical history took place. After three and a half years of work, Dr. Jonas Salk announced that he and his staff had developed a successful vaccine against the dreadful disease. It was a **momentous** occasion and people **rejoiced** upon hearing the news. In some towns, church bells rang, schools closed for the day, and factories stopped for a moment of silence. People **honked their horns**. Department stores announced the news over loudspeakers. One store window displayed the words, "Thank you, Dr. Salk." The announcement was not only a **turning point** in the history of medicine but the moment at which Dr. Jonas Salk became a great medical hero.

4   Jonas Salk was born in 1914 to a lower-middle-class New York family. He was the oldest of three brothers and there was nothing about him as a child to show that he would one day be world famous. Instead, Jonas was a small and thin, quiet and shy boy. He was a good student who liked to read but was not thought to be particularly brilliant. Neither was he very popular with his classmates.

5   Jonas went to the City College of New York thinking he might study law. Instead he discovered his interest in science and medicine, particularly research. In 1939 he received his M.D. at New York University School of Medicine with the help of a scholarship. Then he went to the University of Michigan to study epidemiology, the science of investigating the origin of disease and how it spreads. There were very few of these researchers at the time and the nature of viruses was mostly unknown. Although Salk could have made much more money by practicing medicine, he insisted on **devoting** himself to research. He said, "There is more in life than money."

6   Although Dr. Salk became a great hero and celebrity for his work, he disliked the fame and publicity. He remained **humble** and serious, dedicated to his love of humanity. He **acknowledged** the work of his fellow researchers and of those whose earlier work helped him make his discovery. In 1963 Jonas Salk started the Salk Institute for Biological Studies at La Jolla, California. He gave other scientists the freedom to work there. Meanwhile he dedicated his research to another battle in the fight against cancer.

VOCABULARY

What is the meaning of the underlined words? Circle the letter of the correct answer. Use a dictionary to check your answers.

1. Polio <u>struck</u> the United States in the late 1940s.

   a. attacked

   b. resisted

   c. slowed down

2. Polio <u>crippled</u> 300,000 people.

   a. caused people not to hear anymore

   b. hurt people in a way that they could not use one or more of their limbs

   c. affected their minds so they could not remember things very well

3. Jonas Salk worked seven days a week with his <u>dedicated</u> staff.

   a. specialized

   b. well-known

   c. hardworking

4. When Jonas Salk made his announcement, it was a <u>momentous</u> occasion.

   a. unusual

   b. significant

   c. long-lasting

5. People <u>rejoiced</u> when they heard the great news.

   a. screamed

   b. danced

   c. celebrated

6. People <u>honked their horns</u>.

   a. went into the streets and shouted with joy

   b. jumped up and down

   c. made a sound on their automobile horns

7. The announcement was a <u>turning point</u> in the history of medicine.

   a. time of important change

   b. most enjoyable time

   c. highest point

8. Salk could have practiced medicine but he insisted on <u>devoting</u> himself to research.

   a. encouraging

   b. giving completely

   c. convincing

9. Salk continued to be <u>humble</u> and serious.

   a. ordinary

   b. gentle

   c. modest

10. Salk <u>acknowledged</u> the work of other researchers.

    a. recognized

    b. remembered

    c. checked

COMPREHENSION

A. Skimming for Main Ideas

Circle the letter of the best answer.

1. The main topic of Paragraph 2 is
    a. Salk's development of a successful vaccine.
    b. the dedication of Jonas Salk's staff.
    c. the importance of finding a vaccine for polio.

2. The main topic of Paragraph 3 is how
    a. Salk worked on the vaccine for three and a half years.
    b. people rejoiced as medical history took place.
    c. people liked to celebrate in many different ways.

3. Paragraph 4 is mainly about
    a. Jonas Salk's unpopularity.
    b. Jonas Salk's shyness.
    c. Jonas Salk's childhood.

4. The main topic of Paragraph 5 is that
    a. Salk decided to do research as a career.
    b. Salk was never interested in money.
    c. Salk kept changing his mind about what he wanted to study.

B. Scanning for Details

Scan the paragraphs for details. It is not necessary to read the whole passage again. Some of the following sentences have incorrect facts. Cross out the incorrect fact and write the correct answer above it.

1. Jonas Salk was born in Chicago in 1916.

2. Salk knew the only way to stop the spread of polio was to develop a new method of surgery.

3. Until 1955 there was no cure for polio.

4. Jonas Salk worked alone to find a cure for polio.

5. Salk enjoyed the honors and fame he received after developing a cure for polio.

6. Jonas Salk entered college with the intention of studying law.

7. Instead of practicing medicine as a doctor, Salk devoted himself to research.

8. Salk first tried the polio vaccine on 500 volunteers.

9. Epidemiology is the study of how diseases begin and how they spread.

10. After developing the polio vaccine, Jonas Salk retired.

C. Order of Events

Number the sentences to show the correct order.

_____ Jonas Salk started the Salk Institute.

_____ Salk received his M.D. from New York University.

_____ Salk announced the development of a polio vaccine.

_____ Salk tested the vaccine on his wife and children.

_____ The March of Dimes began a research program at the University of Pittsburgh.

_____ Salk went to the University of Michigan to study epidemiology.

D. Making Inferences and Drawing Conclusions

The answers to these questions are not directly stated in the passage. Circle the letter of the best answer.

1. From the passage, it can be concluded that
   a. Jonas Salk showed all the characteristics of being successful at a young age.
   b. it was Salk's dedication to humanity that was the key to his success.
   c. people have a better chance of being successful if they know what they want to do at a very young age.

2. It can be inferred from the passage that
   a. Salk was less interested in material gain than in helping people through his research.
   b. what made Jonas Salk happy was the fame and recognition he received when he developed the polio vaccine.
   c. Salk did not want to share the glory with anyone else.

3. The passage implies that
   a. people were expecting Salk to develop a vaccine.
   b. people were very grateful for Salk's accomplishment.
   c. there were very few people interested in developing vaccines in those days.

DISCUSSION

Discuss the answers to these questions with your classmates.

1. Do you think people should be prevented from traveling to foreign countries if they have contagious diseases?

2. How are some contagious diseases spread worldwide? What are some ways to prevent the spread of disease?

3. Do you think that modern medicine has made the world a safer place today than it was in the past?

4. Do you think that everybody should be forced to undergo tests for contagious diseases? Should people with these diseases be prevented from going to work or school?

WRITING

Composition: Scientists are presently researching cures for many diseases. Which do you think is the most important disease that a cure should be found for? Give your reasons.

RESEARCH

Find out what medical discovery each of the following scientists is famous for.

1. Crawford W. Long
2. Robert Jarvik
3. Alexander Fleming
4. John Enders
5. Albert Sabin
6. Louis Pasteur
7. Edward Jenner
8. Joseph Lister

TELEVISION COMES TO AMERICA

Unit 18

What TV programs do you like to watch?

How many hours of television do you watch every day?

What is the most popular television program in your country?

1 One of the greatest influences on life in modern America has been television. It affects how Americans dress, talk, relax, vote, and how they view themselves and others. It is one of the most important and powerful inventions of all time.

2 Many Americans can't imagine life without television. Yet it wasn't until the 1950s that television became part of the average American household. As far back as 1879, scientists were looking for ways to add pictures to sound. Inventors worldwide experimented with many types of picture machines. One was called *radiovision*, which used **spinning disks** to transmit pictures. Then in 1922 a 14-year-old American farmboy named Philo T. Farnsworth thought of using electricity **to scan** and transmit pictures.

3 Farnsworth was born in 1906 in a cabin near Beaver, Utah. He worked on his father's farm when he wasn't in school. He was an imaginative boy, very interested in science, especially electricity. When he was still in high school, Farnsworth began experimenting with the idea of using glass tubes and electricity to transmit sound and pictures. After he graduated from college, he found someone to give him money for one year while he experimented with

his idea for television. Just three weeks before the year was over, Farnsworth produced his first TV picture. In 1930, at the age of 24, he was **granted** the first electronic television **patent**.

4   Most major inventions take the combined efforts of many scientists and inventors. In the case of television, a Russian-American named Vladimir Zworykin invented and patented the eye of the television camera and the television screen. For that reason, Zworykin and Farnsworth share the title of "The Fathers of Modern Television."

5   The first televisions were very expensive and still had some problems. Few people had them and broadcasting was extremely limited. But by 1945 television sets began **rolling off** the **assembly lines**. The big radio broadcasting networks began producing television shows. They were funny and entertaining. The news shows were informative. People watched them in store windows and at the homes of neighbors who were lucky enough to own a TV.

6   Soon everyone was saving up to buy a television set. In the beginning of 1950 there were three million television sets in the United States. By the end of the year there were seven million sets. In 1951 it was found that some young people were watching nearly 30 hours of television a week! Television became a **craze**. People couldn't get enough of it. They even started eating meals in front of the television. This gave birth to frozen "TV dinners" in 1954, and "TV trays" to put them on.

7   People were so influenced by television that they copied what they saw and heard. In 1955 the first of three Disney films about the frontiersman, Davy Crockett, was shown. Children and adults loved it. Soon everyone was singing "Davy, Davy Crockett, king of the wild frontier," and everything had a picture of Davy Crockett on it, from pencils to school lunchboxes. Experts started worrying that children were watching too much television and that everyone was being too easily influenced by it. Many predicted it would destroy the family and the American way of life. But the average person didn't care what the experts thought. They loved television and wanted more of it.

8   Today most American families have at least two TV sets. The only activity that takes up more of their free time is sleeping. They are still criticized by some experts for the amount of time they spend in front of the television. But Americans have also proved they are interested in more than entertainment. One of the largest daytime TV audiences in history watched on May 5, 1961, as astronaut Alan Shepard became the first American to take off into space. In 1969 approximately 600 million people worldwide watched astronaut Neil Armstrong take the first step on the moon.

9   As much as Americans like to be entertained, they are also **eager** to be informed. The variety of television programming has expanded greatly over the years. Television has proved it can be a wonderful tool for education. Many stations only show programs on nature, science, music, language, and other educational subjects. News stations keep people informed 24 hours a day. Busy Americans can shop through home-shopping networks. Sports enthusiasts can watch all their favorite games and players.

10   The future of television is only limited by the **pace** of new technology. Sharper images, smaller "boxes," bigger screens, stereo sound, screens within screens, and stop action are all part of our present technology. It will

continue to improve. Televisions will be **linked to** computers tied to our home telephones. They will be part of America's "information superhighway." Hundreds of channels will be available to viewers. Learning, shopping, banking, communicating, as well as entertaining will all be functions of television. The televisions of tomorrow will have voice command, as will computers. Just think. After all these years that televisions have been talking to us, we'll finally have an opportunity to talk back!

VOCABULARY

Complete each definition with one of the following words. Guess your answers, then check with a dictionary.

spinning disks	to scan	patent	eager
granted	assembly line	linked to	
craze	rolling off	pace	

1. The speed or the rate of movement of something is its _____.

2. When something is joined or connected to something else, it is _____ it.

3. When a person is full of interest or desire, he or she is _____.

4. When something becomes a popular fashion, it becomes a _____.

5. A piece of writing from a government office that gives someone the right to make or sell a new invention is called a _____.

6. To put an object under a moving electron beam that converts it to an image that can be transmitted is _____.

7. When something that has been asked for or requested is given, it is _____.

8. When a product goes through a process where it passes from operation to operation in a direct line until it is finished in a mechanically efficient way, it goes through an

_____.

9. When products are _____ an assembly line, they are being manufactured quickly and in large quantities.

10. _____ are thin circular objects that revolve very rapidly.

COMPREHENSION

A. Skimming for Main Ideas

Circle the letter of the best answer.

1. The main topic of Paragraph 3 is about how
   a. Farnsworth was interested in inventions.
   b. Farnsworth produced his first television picture.
   c. the first television patent was given to Farnsworth.

2. Paragraph 7 is mainly about
   a. the influence television had on children and the family.
   b. the popularity of the film *Davy Crockett*.
   c. the experts' warnings that children watched too much television.

3. The main topic of Paragraph 9 is
   a. home-shopping networks on television.
   b. television as a tool for education.
   c. the variety of programs on television.

4. The main topic of the last paragraph is that
   a. future television will have a variety of functions.
   b. televisions will have voice command in the future.
   c. televisions will be linked to computers.

B. Scanning for Details

Find the details to complete these sentences as quickly as possible. It is not necessary to read the whole passage again.

1. "The Fathers of Modern Television" are _____ and

   _____ .

2. When Farnsworth was a high school student, he experimented with using

   _____ and _____ to transmit

   _____ and _____ .

3. Very few people had the first televisions available because they were

   _____ and _____ .

4. Television became part of the average American household during the 19 _____ .

5. When people started eating meals in front of the television, it led to the invention of _____ and _____ .

6. Television has proved that it can be used for _____ as well as entertainment.

7. One of the most popular films in 1955 was about _____ .

8. When people started watching a lot of television, experts warned that it might hurt _____ and _____ .

9. Televisions will continue to improve with new _____ .

10. Televisions and _____ will work together in the future and become part of the "information superhighway."

C. Order of Events

Number the sentences to show the correct order.

_____ Farnsworth was given money to experiment with television for one year.

_____ Radiovision was invented.

_____ Americans started doing their shopping by using home shopping networks on TV.

_____ Six hundred million viewers watched Neil Armstrong step onto the moon.

_____ Farnsworth was granted a patent for his television.

_____ Farnsworth graduated from college.

_____ There were three million television sets in the United States.

D. Making Inferences and Drawing Conclusions

The answers to these questions are not directly stated in the passage. Circle the letter of the best answer.

1. From the passage, it can be concluded that

   a. television was an invention in which people saw only advantages.

   b. it took Americans a long time to begin to appreciate the invention of television.

   c. the invention of television had an effect on American customs.

2. It can be inferred from the passage that

    a. television has developed primarily into a tool for education.

    b. Americans like to have a variety of programs to choose from.

    c. programs showing people traveling into space are the most popular programs on television today.

3. The passage implies that

    a. television will continue to expand its usefulness in the future.

    b. Americans are more interested in watching television than in sleeping.

    c. television programming can't keep up with the development of new technology.

DISCUSSION

Discuss the answers to these questions with your classmates.

1. How do you think television has affected family life?

2. Do you think there's too much violence on television? How do you think it affects people?

3. If you could dictate what is shown on TV, what kinds of programs would you broadcast?

4. Many people believe that future television, which will be combined with computers, will play a significant role in our daily lives. Discuss the advantages and disadvantages of this.

WRITING

Composition: Give two reasons for or against watching television.

RESEARCH

Find out what communication device each of the following people invented.

1. John Logie Baird
2. Johannes Gutenberg
3. Alexander Graham Bell
4. Samuel Morse
5. Guglielmo Marconi
6. Arthur Korn
7. Chester Carlson

THE WRIGHT BROTHERS TAKE OFF

What are some of the ways in which people can fly?

Do you like to fly?

Would you like to own your own airplane?

1   From the time of primitive man, humans have wanted to fly. Centuries ago men **strapped** wings on themselves in an attempt to fly. Needless to say, more than one leg was broken trying that. By 1900, humans had finally succeeded in flying through the air. They had done it in balloons and **gliders**. Now they were ready for the next step.

2   Two brothers, Orville and Wilbur Wright, owned a bicycle shop in Dayton, Ohio, and loved mechanical things. They were also **fascinated** with the idea of flying. They had read about the glider experiments of Otto Lilienthal, a German inventor, and Octave Chanute, a French-born American engineer. They decided to make a glider of their own. They came up with a biplane, or double-wing, glider. It had a new feature called "wing warping," a way of bending the wings to make the best use of air flowing over them. They made several

THE WRIGHT BROTHERS TAKE OFF   *117*

successful flights with their biplane glider. But the Wright brothers wanted more.

3　　They asked the U.S. Weather Bureau where the strongest and steadiest winds blew, which were necessary for glider flying. As Orville and Wilbur and other glider pilots knew, when the winds died down, the plane went down too. In the fall of 1900, the Wright brothers took a new glider to the windy beaches near Kitty Hawk, North Carolina. It had bent wings and a **flap** in front for better up-and-down movement. Once again, their glider was successful. Once again, it wasn't quite good enough.

4　　The Wright brothers went back to their home in Dayton. They set up a wind tunnel to test the data that Lilienthal and Chanute had **come up with** in their glider experiments. The wind tests showed the figures were wrong. The Wright brothers had more designing to do.

5　　In 1902 Orville and Wilbur were back in Kitty Hawk with a redesigned glider. This one had straighter wings, a movable **rudder**, and better control. They made more than a thousand successful flights on the deserted beaches. But the Wright brothers weren't happy with having to rely on nature and its unpredictable winds. They wanted more. They wanted powered flight.

6　　No engine on the market was light and powerful enough for an airplane. So they built their own. There were no **propellers** around either. So they built them too. They put one propeller behind the engine and one behind the pilot. Power from the engine was carried to the propellers by a bicycle chain.

7　　The brothers went back and forth to Kitty Hawk. With each unsuccessful flight, they corrected the problem and tried again. On December 17, 1903, they were ready for another trial. They had named their odd-looking, two-winged **contraption** Flyer. It was a cold, windy day. No one, except four men and a boy, was interested enough to watch the Wright brothers try their funny flying machine. No one believed that humans would ever fly a mechanical plane.

8　　The brothers always took turns at piloting their experimental airplanes. This day, Orville climbed into Flyer and lay flat on the lower wing. He started the engine and the plane moved forward. Then it lifted off the ground, reaching 40 feet. Orville found the controls so sensitive that when he changed the angle of the controls just a little, the plane rose or fell sharply. Then he altered one of the controls a little too much and the plane came down. It had flown 120 feet and had been in the air for 12 seconds. History had been made. What humankind had dreamed about for thousands of years had become reality.

9　　The Wright brothers made three more flights that day. The fourth flight lasted 59 seconds and went a distance of 852 feet. After this flight, everyone gathered around the aircraft. They joyfully discussed what had happened. Suddenly a strong **gust** of wind picked up the plane and turned it over and over while everyone watched in **dismay**. It was badly damaged and could not be flown again that day. But the Wright brothers could not be sad. They had accomplished their goal.

10　　In spite of this great historical achievement, the Wright brothers and their flight went nearly unnoticed. They continued their research and experimentation for almost three more years. Finally, they were granted a U.S. patent on their plane in 1906. In 1907 they went to Europe and flew their aircraft from place to place, to the delight of thousands of Europeans. The success of this tour reached American newspapers. The Wright brothers finally achieved their long-deserved fame and honor. The door was opened to the future. That having been done, it took Americans only 66 years to go from the beaches of Kitty Hawk to the distant moon.

VOCABULARY

What is the meaning of the underlined words? Circle the letter of the correct answer. Use a dictionary to check your answers.

1. A long time ago, men strapped on wings in order to fly.
   a. sewed with thread
   b. fastened with bands
   c. stuck with glue

2. Men had flown in balloons and gliders.
   a. planes without engines
   b. planes attached to balloons
   c. balloons with metal frames

3. The Wright brothers were fascinated with the idea of flying.
   a. very troubled
   b. extremely concerned
   c. very interested

4. The glider had bent wings and a flap in front.
   a. handle
   b. movable edge
   c. wooden support

5. The Wright brothers tested what other inventors had come up with in their experiments.
   a. dreamed about
   b. found out
   c. taken up

6. The glider had a movable rudder.
   a. blade at the back that controls the direction
   b. instrument that indicates speed
   c. seat for the pilot

7. There were no propellers for their airplane.
   a. controls for the pilot
   b. blades that are turned at a high speed by the engine
   c. wings that move up and down mechanically

8. The brothers called their contraption *Flyer*.
   a. small motor
   b. well-designed engine
   c. strange-looking machine

9. A <u>gust</u> of wind picked up the plane.

    a. sudden, strong rush of air

    b. soft breeze

    c. air that swirls like a cyclone

10. People watched in <u>dismay</u>.

    a. alarm

    b. suspicion

    c. delight

COMPREHENSION

A. Skimming for Main Ideas

Circle the letter of the best answer.

1. Paragraph 5 is mainly about

    a. the Wright brothers going back to Kitty Hawk.

    b. the Wright brothers making more than a thousand flights.

    c. the dissatisfaction of the brothers with their glider.

2. Paragraph 6 is mostly about the fact that

    a. the brothers built their own engine and propellers.

    b. many mechanical parts did not exist at that time.

    c. the power from the engine went to the propellers.

3. The main topic of Paragraph 8 is

    a. the *Flyer* went 120 feet on its first flight.

    b. the Wright brothers made an historical achievement.

    c. the controls of the *Flyer* were very sensitive.

4. The last paragraph is mainly about the fact that

    a. the Wright brothers were granted a patent.

    b. the Wright brothers finally got their long-deserved fame.

    c. it took Americans 66 years to go from the beaches of Kitty Hawk to the distant moon.

B. Scanning for Details

Scan the paragraphs for details. It is not necessary to read the whole passage again. Some of the following sentences have incorrect facts. Cross out the incorrect fact and write the correct answer above it.

  1. The Wright brothers discovered that Lilienthal's and Chanute's data were incorrect.

  2. The first plane the Wright brothers made was a single-wing airship.

3. Orville and Wilbur Wright owned a bicycle shop in Dayton, Ohio.

4. The Wright brothers tested their planes at the beach near Kitty Hawk, South Carolina, because there were light, gentle breezes there.

5. The Wright brothers built their own propellers and engine for their plane.

6. "Wing warping" was a way of straightening the wings so the air would flow under them.

7. The Wright brothers put wheels and a cockpit on their plane for better control.

8. The first successful flight of the *Flyer* lasted 10 seconds and went a distance of 200 feet.

9. In 1907 the Wright brothers traveled all over America in their airplane.

10. Only five people watched Orville Wright make flying history on December 17, 1903.

C. Order of Events

Number the sentences to show the correct order.

_____ Orville and Wilbur used a wind tunnel to make tests.

_____ Men strapped wings to their arms in an attempt to fly.

_____ The Wright brothers made over a thousand flights in their glider.

_____ Orville and Wilbur Wright built a glider.

_____ The *Flyer* was damaged.

_____ The Wright brothers made the world's first flight in a motorized plane.

_____ Lilienthal and Chanute experimented with gliders.

_____ The Wright brothers were given a U.S. patent for their plane.

D. Making Inferences and Drawing Conclusions

The answers to these questions are not directly stated in the passage. Circle the letter of the best answer.

1. From the passage, it can be concluded that
   a. fame and fortune came easily to the Wright brothers as a result of their experiments with gliders.
   b. the first flight of the *Flyer* was a great disappointment to the Wright brothers.
   c. the Wright brothers were determined to fly and were willing to work hard to make their dream come true.

2. It can be inferred from the passage that

    a. although the *Flyer* made history with its first successful flight, the Wright brothers still had many improvements to make on its design.

    b. no one had made any achievements in flying until the Wright brothers began their experiments.

    c. very few people had any interest in the idea of flying until 1902 when Orville and Wilbur Wright designed a new glider.

3. The passage implies that

    a. the Europeans were basically responsible for the invention of the motorized plane.

    b. the U.S. Weather Bureau played an important role in the invention of the first glider.

    c. after the Wright brothers flew their motorized plane for the first time, Americans did not appreciate the importance of what they had done.

DISCUSSION

Discuss the answers to these questions with your classmates.

1. Why do you think some people have a fear of flying?

2. How has the invention of jet planes affected our lives?

3. What other inventions in transportation have affected our lives?

4. What do you think passenger planes will be like in the future?

WRITING

Composition: Some people like to travel by train or car. Others like the speed and efficiency of jet flight. What is your favorite form of transportation? Give reasons to support your point of view.

RESEARCH

Find out what form of air travel the following people invented.

1. Joseph and Jacques Montgolfier

2. Henri Giffard

3. Samuel Pierpont Langley

4. Igor Sikorsky

5. Wernher von Braun

6. Christopher Cockerell

7. Sir George Cayley

CULTURE

Part 5

Unit 20
The History of Rock

Unit 21
T-Shirts and Tuxedos

Unit 22
The "Hole" Story About Doughnuts

Unit 23
All-American Football

Unit 24
The Sound of Country Music

THE HISTORY OF ROCK

What rock music singers or groups do you know about?

Is rock music popular in your country?

Do you like rock music? Say why or why not.

1   In 1955, rock and roll was born in America. That year Bill Haley and His Comets performed "Rock Around the Clock," the first big hit of this new style of music. It was first known as "rock and roll" and then simply as "rock." It would become the most popular type of American music from that point on. And it would always appeal to young people as an expression of their search for identity and independence.

2   Rock and roll of the mid-1950s grew mainly out of rhythm and blues. It was a dance music of African-Americans that combined blues, jazz, and gospel styles. Rock was also influenced by country and western music. The most successful early rock and roll performer was Elvis Presley. He **reigned** as the "king" of rock and roll for a decade.

THE HISTORY OF ROCK   125

3   Just as rock and roll **originated** from a combination of music styles, it developed into many different forms. During the 1960s rock music was made up of a number of different styles. It ranged from the surf music of the Beach Boys to the hard rock of the Rolling Stones. One of the big differences between 1960s rock and earlier rock and roll was the use of electronic instruments and sound equipment. It was also freer and more **experimental**.

4   British groups played an important part in the development of rock music in the 1960s. The Beatles were the first British group to **achieve** success in the USA. Their first hit recordings were "I Want to Hold Your Hand," "Can't Buy Me Love," and "Love Me Do." Other successful British groups were the Rolling Stones, The Who, and the Animals. Meanwhile in America, San Francisco was becoming the leading center of rock with such groups as Jefferson Airplane and the Grateful Dead.

5   In the 1970s rock was as popular as ever. Many of the rock groups of the 1960s broke up. Others like the Rolling Stones and Grateful Dead continued to perform and record. The 1970s and early '80s were years of great technological progress in the production of rock music. **Sophisticated** instruments and recording equipment were used, including tape recorders with several tracks, and **synthesizers**. Like the 1960s, the 1970s also saw the development of different styles. Heavy metal used extreme **amplification** and long electric guitar **solos**. Some of the best-known heavy-metal rock performers included Alice Cooper, Grand Funk Railroad, and Aerosmith.

6   The rock music of the late 1970s once again **emphasized** the rhythm and energy of early rock and roll. It also helped produce the styles of the 1980s and '90s. Today rock is still wide open to **diversity**, experimentation, and invention. It is still the music of young people. But today older people who listened to rock when they were young continue to enjoy it. In many ways rock is a mirror of American culture. It is energetic and unpredictable. It is a mixture of styles that work together, and it offers something to people of all ages. It seems Americans will always be rockin' round the clock.

VOCABULARY

What is the meaning of the underlined words? Circle the letter of the correct answer. Use a dictionary to check your answers.

1. Elvis Presley <u>reigned</u> as the "king" of rock and roll for a decade.

   a. won

   b. performed

   c. ruled

2. Rock and roll <u>originated</u> from a combination of music styles.

   a. was introduced

   b. was created

   c. copied

3. Rock music of the 1960s was more <u>experimental</u> than earlier rock and roll.

   a. Things were done the same way as in the past.

   b. One method only was used.

   c. New ways of making music were tried.

4. The Beatles were the first British group to <u>achieve</u> success in the United States.

   a. gain

   b. miss

   c. begin

5. More <u>sophisticated</u> instruments were used in the 1970s.

   a. refined

   b. simple

   c. different

6. <u>Synthesizers</u> were also used in the 1970s.

   a. electric guitars and loudspeakers

   b. electronic instruments with a single sound

   c. electronic keyboards that make many different sounds

7. The heavy-metal music also made use of long electric guitar <u>solos</u>.

   a. many things combined

   b. several different sounds

   c. performances by one member of the group

8. The heavy-metal style of music used extreme <u>amplification</u>.

   a. quiet rhythm

   b. increased volume

   c. fast beat

9. The rock music of the late 1970s <u>emphasized</u> the rhythm of early rock and roll.

   a. gave importance to

   b. forgot

   c. included

10. Rock music today is still open to <u>diversity</u>.

    a. unity

    b. difficulties

    c. differences

COMPREHENSION

A. Skimming for the Main Ideas

Circle the letter of the best answer.

1. Paragraph 1 is mainly about
   a. what rock music means to young people.
   b. the first appearance of rock and roll in America.
   c. the change from "rock and roll" to simply "rock."

2. The main topic of Paragraph 2 is
   a. the life of Elvis Presley as the "king" of rock and roll.
   b. the origin of rock and roll music.
   c. the difference between rock and roll and African dance music.

3. The main topic of Paragraph 4 is
   a. how San Francisco became the center of rock in the 1960s.
   b. the growing popularity of rock music in the 1960s.
   c. the contributions of the British to the development of rock music.

4. The last paragraph is mainly about
   a. the continuing popularity of rock music.
   b. how America is reflected in rock music.
   c. the appeal of rock music to older generations.

B. Scanning for Details

Find the details to complete these sentences as quickly as possible. It is not necessary to read the whole passage again.

1. Early rock and roll was strongly influenced by _____ , a dance music of African-Americans.

2. The most successful early rock and roll performer was _____ .

3. _____ is considered the year that rock and roll was born.

4. The first big hit of the new style of music called rock and roll was

   _____ performed by

   _____ .

5. Unlike early rock and roll, rock music of the 1960s made use of

_____ and sound equipment.

6. During the 1960s _____ became the leading center of rock music.

7. In the 1970s and early 1980s, there was great _____ progress in the production of rock music.

8. Rock music has always appealed to young people because _____

_____ .

9. _____ were the first British rock group to be successful in the United States.

10. The rock music of the late 1970s emphasized _____

_____

and helped produce the rock styles of the 1980s and '90s.

C. Order of Events

Number the sentences to show the correct order.

_____ Synthesizers and sophisticated instruments started being used to produce rock music.

_____ The Beatles made their first hit recordings.

_____ Bill Haley and His Comets performed "Rock Around the Clock."

_____ The first electronic instruments and sound equipment were used.

_____ Elvis Presley became the "king" of rock and roll.

D. Making Inferences and Drawing Conclusions

The answers to these questions are not directly stated in the passage. Circle the letter of the best answer.

1. From the passage, it can be concluded that

　a. groups outside the United States did not have much influence on rock music.

　b. rock music does not appeal to a wide audience.

　c. rock music will continue to change.

2. It can be inferred from the passage that

    a. rock music lost its popularity for a while in the 1970s.

    b. modern inventions had an effect on rock music.

    c. all rock music is loud and energetic.

3. The passage implies that

    a. rock music is not popular outside the United States.

    b. rock music was played in England before it was played in America.

    c. American culture is diverse.

DISCUSSION

Discuss the answers to these questions with your classmates.

1. Give two good or bad influences that rock music has had on people.

2. What other kinds of music do you know?

3. Who is your favorite musician or singer?

4. What do you think the music of the future will be like?

WRITING

Composition: State two ways in which young people are influenced by rock stars. Give specific details to support your ideas.

RESEARCH

Choose a rock artist. Read about his or her life. Find the answers to the following questions.

1. Date of birth   **4.** Greatest influence on career

2. Place of birth   **5.** What artist is famous for

3. When artist started career

T-SHIRTS AND TUXEDOS

Do you like to wear T-shirts?

What do you wear with T-shirts?

When do people wear tuxedos?

1   Styles are constantly changing. Fashions come and go. But few have had the popularity or permanence of the T-shirt and tuxedo. Both of these well-known American garments share a history of French influence and American **daring**.

2   The story of the tuxedo goes back to the summer of 1886, in Tuxedo Park, New York. A Frenchman named Pierre Lorillard was living in the small town. He was **heir to** the Lorillard tobacco fortune and an important New York blueblood, a person of high distinction. Pierre had been invited as always to the Autumn Ball. However, he was tired of wearing the accepted **formal attire** of a coat with **tails**. He wanted something more **informal**. So he asked a tailor to make him several jackets in black without tails. They were modeled after the red riding jackets worn by the British for fox hunting.

3   On the night of the ball, Lorillard was too **timid** to wear one of his tailless dinner jackets. But his son and his young friends were more **bold**. They all put on the jackets and went to the ball. Needless to say, everybody was talking. Some people were shocked by their outfits. Others, however, were quite

interested. They saw how much easier it was to pass the evening in a coat without tails.

4   No doubt, if the tailless coat had been worn by anyone other than a Lorillard, it would never have appeared again. But as Lorillard had so much influence, tailors started copying the informal jackets. After a while, they became standard evening attire. The tuxedo got its name, of course, from the town in which it was born. The name *Tuxedo* came from the native Americans. The Algonquians who had inhabited the area called it *P'tauk-Seet*, meaning "wolf." The colonists changed it to "Tucksito." By 1800, when Pierre Lorillard's grandfather arrived in the area, it had already been changed to Tuxedo. In spite of the original meaning of the word, however, good manners are always expected while wearing one.

5   T-shirts made their entrance much later than tuxedos. But they too took a bit of courage to wear. Once again, the French had a role in the story. It seems the French kept their soldiers cool during World War I by giving them cotton knit undershirts. Meanwhile the Americans were hot and scratchy in their wool underwear. By World War II, the Navy and Army had learned a lesson from the French. The cotton shirt in a T shape became part of the uniform for all soldiers and sailors. After the war, T-shirts came home with the soldiers. By then, all the men were wearing them. But they remained out of sight, as underwear should in polite society.

6   But Hollywood and rebellious young men know no rules. In 1951, actor Marlon Brando wore a T-shirt in the movie *A Streetcar Named Desire*. Everyone talked about it, and the T-shirt became a sort of **trademark** for him. Then in the mid-1950s, the young James Dean performed in *Rebel Without a Cause*. He wore a T-shirt too. Then Elvis Presley hit the screen in his T-shirt. It was too much for young people to ignore. Every boy in town wanted to look like James Dean and Elvis Presley. White T-shirts and **baggy** pants became the "cool," or stylish, thing to wear.

7   The 1960s and another generation of rebellious youth arrived. T-shirts and blue jeans worn by both males and females were their special fashion style. They dyed T-shirts different colors and put pictures and words on them. T-shirts would never be the same again.

8   Today, the T-shirt has made its way to every corner of the world. They're worn by infants, teenagers, and senior citizens. They tell others what we like, where we've been, the things we've done, and races we've won. They can be old and worn, or new and fancy. They can be made of cotton or of silk. They're worn with skirts, pants, and shorts. And something that would have surprised even Lorillard is that T-shirts are even worn with tuxedos.

VOCABULARY

What is the meaning of the underlined words? Circle the letter of the correct answer. Use a dictionary to check your answers.

1. These garments share a history of French influence and American <u>daring</u>.

   a. spirit

   b. bravery

   c. style

2. Pierre Lorillard was <u>heir to</u> a tobacco fortune.

   a. the one who inherits property

   b. the manager of

   c. the father of

3. Pierre Lorillard was tired of wearing <u>formal</u> clothes.

   a. as accepted by rules or customs

   b. old-fashioned

   c. of the latest fashion

4. The accepted <u>attire</u> for the ball was a coat with tails.

   a. costume

   b. clothing

   c. uniform

5. Men wore a coat with <u>tails</u> to the Autumn Ball.

   a. a coat with a long, overlapping collar

   b. a coat with two long lower-back parts

   c. a coat with buttons down both sides of the front

6. Pierre Lorillard wanted to wear something <u>informal</u>.

   a. different

   b. casual

   c. unique

7. Lorillard was too <u>timid</u> to wear his tailless dinner jacket.

   a. lacking in courage

   b. excited

   c. proud

8. His son and his friends were more <u>bold</u>.

   a. dependable

   b. impolite

   c. courageous

9. The T-shirt became a kind of <u>trademark</u> for Marlon Brando.

   a. label

   b. tradition

   c. legend

10. Young people wanted to wear white T-shirts and <u>baggy</u> pants.

    a. loose

    b. tight

    c. short

COMPREHENSION

A. Skimming for Main Ideas

Circle the letter of the best answer.

1. Paragraph 2 is mainly about
   a. how a rich man named Pierre Lorillard lived in a small town.
   b. how the story of the tuxedo began.
   c. what people wore to the Autumn Ball in Tuxedo Park.

2. The main topic in Paragraph 5 is
   a. what soldiers wore during World War I.
   b. how the T-shirt got its name.
   c. when T-shirts started to be worn.

3. The main topic in Paragraph 6 is
   a. how Hollywood made the T-shirt popular.
   b. what Marlon Brando wore in a movie.
   c. why boys wanted to look like Elvis Presley and James Dean.

4. The last paragraph is mainly about
   a. how T-shirts are worn by people of all ages.
   b. the popularity of the T-shirt today.
   c. the different kinds of T-shirts people wear.

B. Scanning for Details

Scan the paragraphs for details. It is not necessary to read the whole passage again. Circle T if the statement is true. Circle F if the statement is false.

1. The word *tuxedo* comes from a Native American word meaning "wolf."　　T　F
2. Pierre Lorillard asked his tailors to make him a tailless jacket to wear when he went hunting.　　T　F
3. Although Pierre Lorillard thought up the idea of the tailless jacket, he wasn't the first person to wear it.　　T　F
4. The first person to wear a T-shirt on the movie screen was James Dean.　　T　F
5. Pierre Lorillard had inherited the family's banking fortune.　　T　F
6. When Lorillard's son and his friends wore the tailless jackets, everyone loved them.　　T　F
7. The T-shirt originated with the French military.　　T　F
8. In the 1960s, colored T-shirts with words printed on them came into style.　　T　F
9. In the 1950s, white T-shirts and baggy pants were the style.　　T　F
10. Pierre Lorillard's grandfather gave Tuxedo Park its name.　　T　F

C. Order of Events

Number the sentences to show the correct order.

_____ Elvis Presley wore a T-shirt in his movies.

_____ Lorillard asked his tailors to make several dinner jackets without tails.

_____ T-shirts became part of the American military uniform.

_____ Pierre Lorillard's grandfather arrived in America.

_____ T-shirts and blue jeans became the fashion.

_____ Tailors began to make copies of Lorillard's tailless jacket.

_____ Lorillard's son wore the tailless jacket to the Autumn Ball.

D. Making Inferences and Drawing Conclusions

The answers to these questions are not directly stated in the passage. Circle the letter of the best answer.

1. From the passage, it can be concluded that
   a. fashions are often started by the military.
   b. most fashions start with large groups of people who wear certain clothing for practical reasons.
   c. fashions often become popular when they are worn by someone people admire.

2. It can be inferred from the passage that
   a. the tuxedo would have been popular no matter who created it.
   b. T-shirts and tuxedos were both ignored when they were worn in public for the first time.
   c. it took the influence of Hollywood to make T-shirts outerwear instead of underwear.

3. The passage implies that
   a. the clothes we wear say something about ourselves.
   b. fashions are often started by people who want to look like everyone else.
   c. new fashions are usually worn by adults before they become popular with young people.

DISCUSSION

Discuss the answers to these questions with your classmates.

1. What is the fashion this year? Do you like it?

2. If you were a fashion designer, what fashion style would you create for next year?

3. If you could print anything you wanted on your T-shirt, what would you put on it?

4. Do you like to wear designer clothes? Why or why not?

WRITING

Composition: Write two reasons for or against wearing the current fashion styles.

RESEARCH

Find out where each of the following garments came from and how they are worn.

1. Stetson   5. Kimono

2. Blue jeans   6. Kilt

3. Sneakers   7. Clogs

4. Loafers

THE "HOLE" STORY ABOUT DOUGHNUTS

Unit 22

Do you like doughnuts?

How many kinds of doughnuts do you think there are?

Which ones do you like the best?

1 Nothing is more American than hot dogs, hamburgers and Cokes—except, of course, sweet doughnuts. Doughnuts may not be served at Fourth of July barbecues but they are on the menu every morning at millions of coffee shops across America. They can be brown with cinnamon, white with powdered sugar, pink with icing, round, long, or twisted. They're **dunked**, licked, **munched** and sometimes **twirled** on a finger. But no matter what shape or flavor they are or how they're eaten, they have a long history of being the USA's favorite breakfast treat.

2 The first doughnut to appear on the American scene would be pretty **stale** by now because it has been around since the beginning of the country's history. The early colonial settlers had a taste for doughnuts and even wrote about them in their historical records. Back then, they were simply fried sweet cakes. Actually doughnuts are a food as old as oil and flour, one of humankind's most ancient and simplest foods. They were made by **grinding** grain into flour, then mixing the flour with water to make the **dough**. Then they fried the dough in oil and poured honey over it to sweeten it. Through the ages, all societies have had some form of this food. Each called it by a different name. This fried cake also took many different shapes around the world. It was round or twisted, and some even had one or more holes.

3 The settlers brought these recipes for fried sweet cakes with them to the New World. What a surprise it was when it turned out the natives had their

own form of doughnut. It was a fried-dough cake of cornmeal, often sweetened with tree sap. A **petrified** doughnut with a hole in the middle was dug up several years ago from a cave in Oklahoma. The cave was full of **relics** from a prehistoric native tribe.

4   It's not certain when the word *doughnut* actually came to be used in America, but it began to appear in recipes during the 18th century. It became a very popular food on the **frontier**. It was a basic and easy meal for settlers traveling west. As time went on, people continued to make doughnuts in their homes and in some bakeries. During World War I, girls who worked for an organization called the Salvation Army fried doughnuts for the soldiers at war in France. They used garbage cans as pots and started with just a few doughnuts. Soon they couldn't keep up with the demand. The soldiers loved them, not only because they filled their stomachs, but because they reminded them of home. When they did go home after the war, they asked for more.

5   A man named Adolph Levitt was there to provide them. He owned a bakery. When he realized the ex-soldiers wanted doughnuts, he put a pot in the window so people could watch the doughnuts fry as a man turned them over with a stick. People loved it. And they loved to eat them too. Eventually Adolph couldn't make enough doughnuts for his customers. He talked to an engineer about making a doughnut machine. After 12 attempts, the Wonderful Almost Human Automatic Donut Machine was invented. This too was put in the bakery window. Again people were fascinated as they watched dough go in and doughnuts **stream out**.

6   Bakeries from all over the country came to buy the machines as doughnut fever hit America. Doughnut shops popped up everywhere. All across the USA, people were making, buying, and eating doughnuts—just like they do today.

VOCABULARY

What is the meaning of the underlined words? Circle the letter of the correct answer. Use a dictionary to check your answers.

1. Doughnuts are <u>dunked</u>.

   a. dipped into sugar while eating

   b. dipped into a liquid while eating

   c. broken into small pieces while eating

2. Doughnuts are <u>munched</u>.

   a. eaten with great movement of the mouth

   b. chewed for a long time

   c. eaten with small bites

3. Doughnuts are sometimes <u>twirled</u> on a finger.

   a. pushed up and down

   b. turned around and around

   c. thrown into the air

4. The first doughnut that appeared in America would be <u>stale</u> today.

   a. prehistoric

   b. not fresh

   c. unique

5. They were made by <u>grinding</u> grain into flour.

   a. crushing into a powder

   b. pressing into a powder

   c. beating into a powder

6. They mixed the flour with water to make the <u>dough</u>.

   a. liquid mixture made with flour and water

   b. soft, pasty mass made with flour and water

   c. light, fluffy food made with flour and water

7. A <u>petrified</u> doughnut with a hole in the middle was found in a cave in Oklahoma.

   a. turned into stone

   b. rooted

   c. soft and rotted

8. The cave had <u>relics</u> from a prehistoric tribe.

   a. remains

   b. souvenirs

   c. traces

9. Doughnuts became popular on the <u>frontier</u>.

   a. wild areas of the United States

   b. between the settled and wild areas of the United States

   c. settled areas of the United States

10. People liked to watch the dough go in and doughnuts <u>stream out</u> of the doughnut machine.

    a. rise out of

    b. jump out now and then

    c. come out continuously

COMPREHENSION

A. Skimming for Main Ideas

Circle the letter of the best answer.

1. The main topic in Paragraph 1 is that
   a. doughnuts are America's favorite breakfast treat.
   b. people eat doughnuts in different ways.
   c. doughnuts can have different shapes and flavors.

2. Paragraph 2 is mainly about
   a. how the doughnut takes different shapes around the world.
   b. how the early settlers made doughnuts.
   c. how doughnuts have existed for a long time.

3. The main topic of Paragraph 3 is
   a. the existence of doughnuts in the New World before the settlers.
   b. the petrified doughnut found in a cave.
   c. the remains found in a cave in Oklahoma.

4. Paragraph 5 is mainly about
   a. the fun of cooking doughnuts in a bakery window.
   b. the popularity of Adolph Levitt's doughnuts and his doughnut machine.
   c. the attempts made by Adolph Levitt and an engineer to make a doughnut machine.

B. Scanning for Details

Scan the paragraphs for details. It is not necessary to read the whole passage again. Some of the following sentences have incorrect facts. Cross out the incorrect fact and write the correct answer above it.

1. The word *doughnut* began to appear in American recipes during the 18th century.

2. Adolph Levitt and an engineer were responsible for the invention of the first doughnut machine.

3. The doughnut is one of the oldest and simplest foods.

4. All societies called doughnuts by the same name.

5. The early colonial settlers were familiar with doughnuts as fried sweet cakes.

6. During World War II, girls working for the USO made doughnuts for the soldiers.

7. A petrified doughnut was found in a cave in Tennessee.

8. The Native Americans used sugarcane to sweeten their form of doughnut.

9. Adolph Levitt couldn't keep up with the demand for doughnuts at his bakery.

10. The doughnut was an unusual treat for the American settlers traveling east.

C. Order of Events

Number the sentences to show the correct order.

_____ Doughnut shops appear all across America.

_____ Fried sweet cakes are eaten often by the settlers on the frontier.

_____ The word *doughnut* begins to appear in American recipes.

_____ The settlers bring recipes for fried sweet cakes with them to America.

_____ Girls fry doughnuts for the American soldiers.

_____ The Wonderful Almost Human Automatic Donut Machine is invented.

D. Making Inferences and Drawing Conclusions

The answers to these questions are not directly stated in the passage. Circle the letter of the best answer.

1. From the passage, it can be concluded that
   a. people didn't develop a liking for doughnuts until they were made for the soldiers.
   b. doughnuts in one form or another have been eaten by people for thousands of years.
   c. it's thanks to Adolph Levitt that doughnuts are eaten in America today.

2. It can be inferred from the passage that
   a. the settlers learned how to make doughnuts from the Native Americans.
   b. doughnuts were a basic food eaten by both the natives and the settlers.
   c. doughnuts were prepared and eaten only by advanced civilizations.

3. The passage implies that
   a. the soldiers of World War I ate doughnuts because they were starving.
   b. the doughnut machine didn't have an effect on the popularity of doughnuts.
   c. today's doughnuts come in a greater variety than they did in colonial days.

DISCUSSION

Discuss the answers to these questions with your classmates.

1. Name some breakfast or snack foods that are popular in your country and explain how they are eaten.

2. Almost all foods in supermarkets have preservatives. Do you think this is good or bad?

3. Do you think most people in your country eat a healthy diet? Give reasons.

4. What is your favorite food? Is it good or bad for you?

WRITING

Composition: Describe a custom in your country where a special sweet food or dessert is prepared and eaten.

RESEARCH

Find out where these foods originated.

1. Hamburger   4. Croissant

2. Spaghetti   5. Coffee

3. Bologna

ALL-AMERICAN FOOTBALL

Unit 23

What is the most popular sport in your country?

What do you know about American football?

Do you like football?

1. Football is not just a game in America. It's an event. A *big* event. Millions of people attend football games or watch them on television. Thousands of others play football themselves, on professional, school, or neighborhood teams, or just with friends. The games are often only a part of the colorful spectacles that go with them. Parades and marching bands, cheerleaders, and cheering fans with **banners** and horns are all part of the festivity surrounding football.

2. Football has its beginnings in soccer and rugby. All have the same objective, which is to get the ball to the **opponent's** goal and score points. Soccer was played in England in the 11th century. The ball was advanced only

by kicking it. In 1839 rugby was born when a frustrated English soccer player picked up the ball and ran down the field with it. Soccer was played by American college students in the 1800s, but the game was called "football." Then, in 1874, a new form of the football game developed that combined both soccer and rugby. Players not only kicked the ball but advanced it by running with it and passing it to teammates.

3   American football developed into a rough **contact sport**. Because protective equipment was not used in those days, it was quite dangerous. In 1905, 18 players were killed and 159 seriously injured. President Roosevelt threatened **to ban** football if the roughness didn't stop. The rules committee began changing the rules and eventually football developed into the game it is today.

The basic idea of football is very simple. The team that has the ball runs with it or throws or kicks it toward the other team's goal. Each time the team reaches the other's goal, it scores a certain number of points. The other team tries to stop them. They want to get the ball so they can score. The team that scores the most points wins the game.

4   The teams play for one hour, divided into four quarters. There is always a halftime break of at least 15 minutes. The teams are allowed timeouts, which are times when the clock is stopped and the team can get together to talk about **strategy**. The clock is also stopped when players are injured and when there are penalties given out for playing against the rules. Sometimes new players are **substituted** for those who have already played. There are also breaks for television commercials. With all this going on, the one-hour game can easily take up to two and a half or three hours!

5   Football in the United States is played by more than 600 colleges and universities. The stadiums in which they play are often called "bowls." At the end of the college season, usually in December or January, the best college teams are invited to play against each other in "bowl games." There is the Orange Bowl in Miami, the Sugar Bowl in New Orleans, the Cotton Bowl in Dallas, and the Gator Bowl in Jacksonville, Florida. These games attract large crowds and offer colorful marching bands and **squads** of cheerleaders who perform a combination of gymnastics, dancing, and **drills** to entertain the audience and encourage the players.

6   The greatest of all the bowl games is the Rose Bowl held in Pasadena, California, since 1902. It attracts a crowd of over 100,000 people every year. It is played on New Year's Day. The game itself, however, is not the main attraction. What thousands of people come to see and millions more watch on their televisions internationally is the Tournament of Roses Parade. It is a breathtaking parade of **floats** covered entirely with flowers, petals, seeds, and other flower parts. Marching bands and floats from around the world participate and compete for prizes for the best and most beautiful float. There are circus scenes and tropical forests and giant spaceships, all covered with flowers. The parade is a spectacle of beauty that is unequaled anywhere.

7   After the Rose Bowl and the end of the college football season, fans turn their attention to the professional teams who are playing their own championship games. The final play-off game to decide the season's champion team is called the Super Bowl.

8　　Once again, the game is less important than all the activity surrounding it. It has now become a tradition to have "Super Bowl parties" on "Super Bowl Sunday." Usually, friends gather at one household. Everyone brings food. Some party goers bring extra televisions that are placed outdoors and in rooms throughout the house. That way the guests, in between eating and talking, can watch the game from wherever they are.

9　　Even those not interested in football look forward to seeing the halftime show. This has become quite an **extravaganza.** In recent years, top entertainers have performed at the Super Bowl. Light shows and fireworks displays, marching bands, cheerleaders, and dancers, are all part of halftime. It is watched by millions of viewers around the country. Part sport, part entertainment, football has become an important part of the American way of life.

VOCABULARY

Complete each definition with one of the following words or phrases. Guess your answers, then check with a dictionary.

banners	opponent	strategy	squads
extravaganza	floats	to ban	
substituted	drills	contact sport	

1. A sport in which the players touch each other is a _____.

2. The person who takes the opposite side is the _____.

3. _____ is to forbid something, usually by law.

4. An _____ is an elaborate, spectacular form of entertainment.

5. When something or someone is put in place of another, it is _____.

6. Groups of people working in teams are _____.

7. _____ is skillful planning.

8. Long pieces of cloth on which words or signs are painted are _____.

9. _____ are exercises that a team has been trained to do together.

10. _____ are large, flat vehicles showing special scenes or shows and that are drawn in a procession.

COMPREHENSION

A. Skimming for Main Ideas

Circle the letter of the best answer.

1. Paragraph 2 is mainly about
   a. how football originated from soccer and rugby.
   b. how soccer was played by American college students.
   c. how football is similar to rugby.

2. The main topic in Paragraph 3 is that
   a. American football did not have special equipment.
   b. American football was a rough sport.
   c. President Roosevelt did not like football.

3. Paragraph 5 is mainly about
   a. the entertainment provided at the stadiums.
   b. the large crowds at the bowls.
   c. football games played by colleges and universities.

4. The main topic of the last paragraph is that
   a. top entertainers want to perform at the Super Bowl.
   b. football games are only watched by sports fans.
   c. football today has also become a form of entertainment.

B. Scanning for Details

Find the details as quickly as possible and circle the letter of the correct answer. It is not necessary to read the whole passage again.

1. In football, the team with the ball tries to get it
   a. in a basket.
   b. over their goal.
   c. to the other team's goal.

2. President Roosevelt threatened to stop football because it was getting too
   a. popular.
   b. dangerous.
   c. noisy.

3. Football originated with
   a. basketball.
   b. soccer.
   c. baseball.

4. A football game is divided into
   a. two halves.
   b. three thirds.
   c. four quarters.

5. The stadiums in which football games are held are often called
   a. bowls.
   b. rinks.
   c. coliseums.

6. Along with football games, there are often
   a. circuses.
   b. races.
   c. marching bands.

7. The final play-off game for professional teams is the

   a. Gator Bowl.

   b. Super Bowl.

   c. Rose Bowl.

8. Rugby was started in England in

   a. 1839.

   b. 1874. .

   c. 1905.

9. The Rose Bowl is played on

   a. the first day of the season.

   b. a Sunday.

   c. New Year's Day.

10. During timeouts

   a. the team discusses strategy.

   b. the cheerleaders perform.

   c. the rules are sometimes changed.

C. Order of Events

Number the sentences to show the correct order.

_____ Rugby was born when an English soccer player ran with the ball.

_____ Football developed into a rough sport.

_____ The Super Bowl became a popular American event.

_____ New rules were applied to the game of football.

_____ A new form of game developed in America that combined soccer and rugby.

_____ Soccer was played in England in the 11th century.

D. Making Inferences and Drawing Conclusions

The answers to these questions are not directly stated in the passage. Circle the letter of the best answer.

1. From the passage, it can be concluded that

   a. football will eventually lose its popularity in America.

   b. modern football is as much a form of entertainment as it is a sports event.

   c. football is more popular as a college sport than as a professional sport.

2. It can be inferred from the passage that

   a. the use of protective equipment makes the modern game of football more interesting to watch.

   b. the game of modern football is not much different from the rugby played by American college students many years ago.

   c. soccer, football, and rugby have several common elements.

3. The passage implies that

  a. football often brings Americans together in social situations.

  b. if it weren't for professional teams, football wouldn't be popular in America.

  c. football games are usually watched by people who are athletes themselves.

DISCUSSION

Discuss the answers to these questions with your classmates.

1. What customs are associated with sports in your country?

2. Do you think professional athletes should be paid such high salaries?

3. Who is your favorite sports star? Why?

4. Do you think professional players should be allowed to participate in the Olympics?

WRITING

Composition: Why are sports so popular? Give two examples of popular sports and why people like them.

RESEARCH

For the sports of ice hockey, tennis, judo, basketball, and soccer, find out the following facts.

1. The number of players on a team

2. The uniforms that are worn

3. The kind of equipment that is used

4. How the game is scored

THE SOUND OF COUNTRY MUSIC

Do you like songs about love and heartache?

What famous country music singers do you know?

Do you like country music? Explain why or why not.

1   Put together a guitar, singer, simple music, and **sentimental** words, and you've got country music. The sound is uniquely American. But like so much in this land of immigrants, it's a combination of the past and the present, the borrowed and invented. Its deepest roots are in faraway places, in the music brought here by people seeking a new life. The people changed over time and

so did country music. But it has never lost its special sound. Like jazz and early rock and roll, country music is the music of America. It **reflects** the hearts and minds and soul of its people.

2   The history of country music is hundreds of years old. It is older than America itself. It begins with the immigrants from Scotland and Ireland who brought their traditional songs and instruments to the New World. Many went to a southeastern mountain area called Appalachia. These settlers played their bagpipes (a wind instrument) and lutes (pear-shaped stringed instruments). They sang the songs and ballads of their homelands. Eventually, however, the **lyrics** changed. There were new stories to tell, new troubles and heartaches **to mourn**. There were also new loves to sing about. New instruments started to be used too. They were stringed instruments such as zithers, fiddles, guitars, and banjos.

3   As the settlers spread to the south and west, the music of Appalachia went with them. It changed form slightly with the new **environments** and new influences. It gave birth to what became known as country music. This was the real folk music of **rural** America. It was a basic, simple music with songs about love and **grief**, heartache and dying. It was sung at family gatherings and on back **porches**. But eventually it was recorded and heard on radios in the South.

4   People continued to migrate west to California from Oklahoma and Texas. They also went north to cities like Detroit, Chicago, Cleveland, and Baltimore. Again, they took their music with them. Then there were new songs about life in the city and about the railroads that brought them there and connected them with their lives "back home." These songs had titles like "Dallas," "Streets of Baltimore," "Saginaw, Michigan," and "New York City Blues." Time went by and cities and towns spread out across America. New influences continued to change country music. It was recorded, performed, and heard in more and more places.

5   Today, the sound of country music can be heard throughout the land. It has **incorporated** many styles of music like jazz, rock and roll, even Mexican and Hawaiian music. Songs have a much broader range of subjects. However, love and heartache, as in most popular music, are sung about the most. Some people don't like these changes. They think country music isn't "pure" anymore, that it's gone too far from its original sound. But music of all kinds has always been a reflection of society. Since its mountain beginnings, country music has shown the changing face of America, the **transitions** from one generation to another. Times have changed and so has country music. If anything, it's more popular than ever, yet it remains a truly American sound.

VOCABULARY

Complete the definition with one of the following words. Guess your answers, then check with a dictionary.

sentimental	reflects	porches	rural
lyrics	to mourn	grief	
environments	incorporated	transitions	

1. _____ means relating to the country or country life.

2. _____ is the feeling of sadness or suffering at the death of a person.

3. Things that are _____ show a lot of emotion and tenderness based on feeling and not on reason.

4. Something that expresses or gives an idea _____ .

5. _____ are covered entrances to houses, with floors and roofs but no outside walls.

6. _____ is to feel or show grief or sadness, especially over the death of someone.

7. Movements from one state or form to another are _____ .

8. The words of a song are the _____ .

9. The natural or social conditions in which people live are their _____ .

10. When things have been made part of a group or included, they are

   _____ .

COMPREHENSION

A. Skimming for Main Ideas

Circle the letter of the best answer.

1. Paragraph 2 is mainly about
    a. the instruments used in country music.
    b. the beginning of country music by settlers in Appalachia.
    c. the history of the songs that were sung in Scotland and Ireland.

2. The main topic of Paragraph 3 is that

  a. the music of the mountains changed to become country music.

  b. country music was mainly about love.

  c. country music was sung at home.

3. The main topic of Paragraph 4 is

  a. city life had little influence on country music.

  b. the titles of songs became more varied in country music.

  c. country music changed as people moved to cities.

4. The last paragraph is mainly about

  a. how country music has changed today.

  b. why people do not like the country music of today.

  c. how today's country music is influenced by rock and roll.

B. Scanning for Details

Scan the paragraphs for details. It is not necessary to read the whole passage again. Some of the following sentences have incorrect facts. Cross out the incorrect fact and write the correct answer above it.

  1. Country music originated with immigrants from France and Spain.

  2. Country music changed as people migrated to new places.

  3. Country music began as the folk music of urban America.

  4. Modern country music is a combination of many styles, including jazz and rock and roll.

  5. The area in which country music was born is a southwestern mountain area called the Rockies.

  6. The immigrants brought bagpipes and lutes with them to America.

  7. Eventually both the song lyrics and the instruments changed.

  8. Country music changed as America changed.

  9. The most popular subjects in country music have always been dreams and happiness.

  10. Some people think country music hasn't changed enough over the years.

C. Order of Events

Number the sentences to show the correct order.

_____ Immigrants played songs and ballads from their homelands.

_____ Songs began to be recorded and broadcast on radio.

_____ Country music used a mixture of styles and became popular throughout the United States.

_____ Settlers began to use new types of instruments such as fiddles and banjos.

_____ Settlers moved to the south and west and took their music with them.

_____ People moved into cities and new influences continued to change country music.

D. Making Inferences and Drawing Conclusions

The answers to these questions are not directly stated in the passage. Circle the letter of the best answer.

1. From the passage, it can be concluded that

   a. the origins of country music are with ordinary people in a home setting.

   b. country music was created by professional immigrant musicians looking for a new sound. .

   c. if it weren't for jazz and rock and roll, America may never have had country music.

2. It can be inferred from the passage that

   a. country music was a complicated music form that only a few people could compose and play.

   b. early country music songs had no relationship to the songs and instruments brought to the New World by immigrants.

   c. as country music developed in America, it increased its range of subjects and sounds.

3. The passage implies that

   a. country music today still uses a limited number of basic, simple instruments.

   b. some people think country music shouldn't be combined with other music styles.

   c. country music was instantly popular throughout America after it was introduced by immigrants.

DISCUSSION

Discuss the answers to these questions with your classmates.

1. What musical instrument or instruments are special to your country? Describe the instrument and the sound it makes.

2. If you had an opportunity to learn any musical instrument, which would you choose? Why?

3. What lyrics or subjects do you like to hear in songs?

4. What are your favorite popular songs?

WRITING

Composition: What kind of music is native to your country? Name two occasions and/or places when it is played.

RESEARCH

Below is a list of six different types of American music. For each type of music, give the name of one outstanding performer.

1. Gospel   4. Country

2. Blues   5. Folk

3. Jazz   6. Rock

ANSWER KEY

Part 1: People

Unit 1
Vocabulary: **1.** stamina **2.** frigid
3. kennel **4.** sled dog team
5. skidded off **6.** vigorous **7.** trail
8. grueling **9.** untangled
10. desperately
Skimming for Main Ideas: **1.** a
2. b **3.** c **4.** a
Scanning for Details: **1.** 3,000/
1,000 **2.** 1940/1925; Anchorage/
Nome **3.** went to college to become
a veterinarian/began to train and run
dogs for a racing kennel **4.** Correct
5. measles/diphtheria; they couldn't
find a pilot/it was too stormy
6. Correct **7.** Correct **8.** someone
offered her a job/reading about the
Iditarod race in a magazine
9. Correct **10.** the doctor who sent
for the medicine/one of the towns it
passes through
Order of Events: 3, 5, 2, 1, 6, 7, 4
*Making Inferences and Drawing
Conclusions:* **1.** b **2.** a **3.** a

Unit 2
Vocabulary: **1.** b **2.** a **3.** c **4.** b
5. c **6.** a **7.** b **8.** a **9.** c **10.** b
Skimming for Main Ideas: **1.** b
2. a **3.** c **4.** a
Scanning for Details:
1. Milwaukee, Wisconsin **2.** to read
and write **3.** seven **4.** a special
center for troubled girls
5. television talk show hosts **6.** her
father **7.** *The Color Purple; Native
Son* **8.** Tennessee State University
9. news broadcaster **10.** witty;
charming; warm
Order of Events: 7, 3, 1, 4, 5, 2, 6
*Making Inferences and Drawing
Conclusions:* **1.** b **2.** b **3.** b

Unit 3
Vocabulary: **1.** unsuspecting
2. galaxy **3.** talents **4.** sequel
5. break **6.** special effects
7. legend **8.** forces **9.** Sneaked
10. captured the imagination
Skimming for Main Ideas: **1.** a
2. a **3.** b **4.** c
Scanning for Details: **1.** a **2.** b
3. b **4.** c **5.** a **6.** b **7.** c **8.** a
9. c **10.** a
Order of Events: 6, 1, 5, 3, 2, 4
*Making Inferences and Drawing
Conclusions:* **1.** c **2.** c **3.** b

Unit 4
Vocabulary: **1.** b **2.** a **3.** c **4.** b
5. a **6.** b **7.** c **8.** a **9.** c **10.** a
Skimming for Main Ideas: **1.** b
2. b **3.** c **4.** a
Scanning for Details: **1.** F **2.** T
3. F **4.** T **5.** F **6.** F **7.** T **8.** T
9. F **10.** T

Order of Events: 4, 1, 5, 7, 2, 6, 3
*Making Inferences and Drawing
Conclusions:* **1.** a **2.** a **3.** c

Unit 5
Vocabulary: **1.** a **2.** b **3.** c **4.** c
5. b **6.** b **7.** c **8.** a **9.** a **10.** c
Skimming for Main Ideas: **1.** a
2. b **3.** a **4.** c
Scanning for Details: **1.** Kansas
State **2.** 12; McNeil Island
3. canaries **4.** engineering; music;
mathematics **5.** third-grade **6.** all
his birds, books, and personal
property **7.** mother; Woodrow
Wilson **8.** on a rocky island in San
Francisco Bay **9.** life in solitary
confinement **10.** the diseases of
birds
Order of Events: 4, 2, 6, 1, 3, 5, 7
*Making Inferences and Drawing
Conclusions:* **1.** a **2.** b **3.** a

Unit 6
Vocabulary: **1.** contribution
2. jammed **3.** soared
4. underprivileged **5.** suspended
6. renown **7.** reputation
8. pitcher **9.** home run **10.** major-
league
Skimming for Main Ideas: **1.** a
2. b **3.** c **4.** b
Scanning for Details:
1. T **2.** T **3.** F **4.** F **5.** F **6.** T
7. F **8.** T **9.** F **10.** T
Order of Events: 7, 2, 4, 1, 5, 6, 3
*Making Inferences and Drawing
Conclusions:* **1.** a **2.** b **3.** a

Part 2: Places

Unit 7
Vocabulary: **1.** Timber
2. Eccentric **3.** on record **4.** vast
5. Reefs **6.** thaws **7.** Mosses
8. range **9.** spectacular
10. natural phenomenon
Skimming for Main Ideas: **1.** b
2. a **3.** c **4.** a
Scanning for Details: **1.** "Great
Land"; Aleut **2.** Kodiak **3.** tundra
4. the "Land of the Midnight Sun"
5. native peoples; descendants of
the early settlers **6.** Mount
McKinley; 20,320 **7.** aurora borealis;
northern lights **8.** 100,000; 3,000
9. plane; much of Alaska doesn't
have roads **10.** Siberia
Order of Events: 4, 2, 1, 3
*Making Inferences and Drawing
Conclusions:* **1.** b **2.** c **3.** b

Unit 8
Vocabulary: **1.** c **2.** a **3.** c **4.** a
5. b **6.** b **7.** b **8.** a **9.** a **10.** a
Skimming for Main Ideas: **1.** a
2. b **3.** b **4.** a
Scanning for Details: **1.** T **2.** T

3. F **4.** F **5.** F **6.** F **7.** F **8.** T
9. F **10.** F
Order of Events: 4, 6, 1, 3, 7, 2, 5
*Making Inferences and Drawing
Conclusions:* **1.** a **2.** c **3.** c

Unit 9
Vocabulary: **1.** amphibians
2. Burrows **3.** searing **4.** Salt flats
5. Shrubs **6.** devoid of **7.** Harsh
8. Pioneers **9.** precious
10. lodged
Skimming for Main Ideas: **1.** a
2. a **3.** b **4.** c
Scanning for Details; **1.** c **2.** a
3. c **4.** b **5.** a **6.** a **7.** b **8.** b
9. c **10.** b
Order of Events: 3, 1, 4, 2, 5
*Making Inferences and Drawing
Conclusions:* **1.** a **2.** c **3.** c

Unit 10
Vocabulary: **1.** c **2.** a **3.** b **4.** b
5. a **6.** c **7.** a **8.** c **9.** c **10.** a
Skimming for Main Ideas: **1.** a
2. b **3.** c **4.** a
Scanning for Details: **1.** Correct
2. wrote their own/developed the
art of storytelling **3.** French/native;
dark and mysterious/"land of the
trembling earth" **4.** Correct
5. advanced/primitive; often had
contact with/were isolated from
6. Correct **7.** park/wildlife refuge
(or preserve) **8.** Correct
9. difficult and harsh/carefree and
comfortable **10.** all the wild
animals were still living there/some
of the animals had become extinct
Order of Events: 5, 3, 7, 1, 4, 2, 6
*Making Inferences and Drawing
Conclusions:* **1.** b **2.** c **3.** a

Unit 11
Vocabulary: **1.** b **2.** b **3.** b **4.** c
5. a **6.** b **7.** a **8.** b **9.** a **10.** a
Skimming for Main Ideas: **1.** b
2. a **3.** c **4.** b
Scanning for Details: **1.** F **2.** F
3. T **4.** F **5.** T **6.** T **7.** F **8.** T
9. F **10.** F
Order of Events: 2, 5, 1, 7, 3, 6, 4
*Making Inferences and Drawing
Conclusions:*
1. b **2.** b **3.** a

Part 3: Living Things

Unit 12
Vocabulary: **1.** chip **2.** abundant
3. trunk **4.** aroma **5.** tedious
6. clusters **7.** grove **8.** nourishing
9. cultivated **10.** Spouts
Skimming for Main Ideas: **1.** b
2. b **3.** a **4.** b
Scanning for Details: **1.** mokuks
2. sugar **3.** 75 to 100 feet **4.** the
meat of the pecan nut is rich and

nourishing **5.** the central southern area of the United States **6.** the days are warm but the nights are cold **7.** tapping **8.** boiled **9.** 75 to 100 **10.** 25 to 30
Order of Events: 6, 4, 1, 3, 2, 5
Making Inferences and Drawing Conclusions: **1.** b **2.** a **3.** b

Unit 13
Vocabulary: **1.** b **2.** a **3.** c **4.** a **5.** b **6.** a **7.** a **8.** c **9.** b **10.** c
Skimming for Main Ideas: **1.** a **2.** b **3.** c **4.** b
Scanning for Details: **1.** T **2.** T **3.** F **4.** F **5.** F **6.** T **7.** F **8.** F **9.** T **10.** F
Order of Events: 1, 4, 5, 3, 2
Making Inferences and Drawing Conclusions: **1.** a **2.** c **3.** a

Unit 14
Vocabulary: **1.** b **2.** a **3.** c **4.** a **5.** b **6.** a **7.** c **8.** b **9.** a **10.** b
Skimming for Main Ideas: **1.** c **2.** b **3.** b **4.** a
Scanning for Details: **1.** b **2.** a **3.** b **4.** a **5.** c **6.** c **7.** a **8.** a **9.** b **10.** c
Order of Events: 2, 1, 4, 3
Making Inferences and Drawing Conclusions: **1.** c **2.** a **3.** c

Unit 15
Vocabulary: **1.** b **2.** a **3.** c **4.** a **5.** b **6.** a **7.** b **8.** c **9.** c **10.** a
Skimming for Main Ideas: **1.** a **2.** a **3.** b **4.** c
Scanning for Details: **1.** ~~dark red~~/white **2.** Correct **3.** Correct **4.** ~~alone~~/in groups (packs) **5.** ~~three-year old~~/parent **6.** ~~anger~~/closeness as a group **7.** Correct **8.** Correct **9.** ~~use up the food supply~~/keep the balance of nature **10.** ~~large, healthy~~/sick or weak
Order of Events: 4, 3, 1, 2
Making Inferences and Drawing Conclusions: **1.** c **2.** a **3.** b

Part 4: Great Moments

Unit 16
Vocabulary: **1.** collapsible **2.** lunar **3.** living quarters **4.** Gravity **5.** barren **6.** set foot **7.** Ferries **8.** rugged **9.** craft **10.** Drifted
Skimming for Main Ideas: **1.** a **2.** c **3.** b **4.** b
Scanning for Details: **1.** Giovanni Riccioli; telescope **2.** lunar rover; moon buggy **3.** the Sea of Tranquility **4.** *Apollo 17* **5.** gray rock and gray, powder-like soil **6.** moon base **7.** 212 degrees Fahrenheit; boil water **8.** sound travels on air and there is no air on the moon **9.** six times less **10.** it was damaged by an explosion on the way
Order of Events: 3, 5, 1, 4, 2, 6
Making Inferences and Drawing Conclusions: **1.** c **2.** a **3.** b

Unit 17
Vocabulary: **1.** a **2.** b **3.** c **4.** b **5.** c **6.** c **7.** a **8.** b **9.** c **10.** a
Skimming for Main Ideas: **1.** a **2.** b **3.** c **4.** a
Scanning for Details:
1. ~~Chicago~~/New York; ~~1916~~/1914
2. ~~new method of surgery~~/vaccine
3. Correct **4.** ~~alone~~/with a dedicated staff **5.** ~~enjoyed~~/disliked **6.** Correct **7.** Correct **8.** ~~500 volunteers~~/himself **9.** Correct **10.** ~~retired~~/started the Salk Institute and dedicated his research to cancer
Order of Events: 6, 1, 5, 4, 3, 2
Making Inferences and Drawing Conclusions: **1.** b **2.** a **3.** b

Unit 18
Vocabulary: **1.** pace **2.** linked to **3.** eager **4.** craze **5.** patent **6.** to scan **7.** granted **8.** assembly line **9.** rolling off **10.** Spinning disks
Skimming for Main Ideas: **1.** b **2.** a **3.** c **4.** a
Scanning for Details: **1.** Philo T. Farnsworth; Vladimir Zworykin **2.** glass tubes; electricity; sound; pictures **3.** expensive; still had some problems **4.** 50s **5.** TV dinners; TV trays **6.** education **7.** Davy Crockett **8.** the family; the American way of life **9.** technology **10.** computers
Order of Events: 3, 1, 7, 6, 4, 2, 5
Making Inferences and Drawing Conclusions: **1.** c **2.** b **3.** a

Unit 19
Vocabulary: **1.** b **2.** a **3.** c **4.** b **5.** b **6.** a **7.** b **8.** c **9.** a **10.** a
Skimming for Main Ideas: **1.** c **2.** a **3.** b **4.** b
Scanning for Details: **1.** Correct **2.** ~~single-wing airship~~/double-wing glider **3.** Correct **4.** ~~South~~/North; ~~light, gentle breezes~~/strong, steady winds **5.** Correct **6.** ~~straightening~~/bending; ~~under~~/over **7.** ~~wheels~~/a flap; ~~cockpit~~/movable rudder **8.** ~~10~~/12; ~~200~~/120 **9.** ~~America~~/Europe **10.** Correct
Order of Events: 4, 1, 5, 3, 7, 6, 2, 8
Making Inferences and Drawing Conclusions: **1.** c **2.** a **3.** c

Part 5: Culture

Unit 20
Vocabulary: **1.** c **2.** b **3.** c **4.** a **5.** a **6.** c **7.** c **8.** b **9.** a **10.** c
Skimming for Main Ideas: **1.** b **2.** b **3.** c **4.** a
Scanning for Details: **1.** rhythm and blues **2.** Elvis Presley **3.** 1955 **4.** "Rock Around the Clock"; Bill Haley and His Comets **5.** electronic instruments **6.** San Francisco **7.** technological **8.** it's an expression of their search for identity and independence **9.** The Beatles **10.** the rhythm and energy of early rock and roll

Order of Events: 5, 4, 1, 3, 2
Making Inferences and Drawing Conclusions: **1.** c **2.** b **3.** c

Unit 21
Vocabulary: **1.** b **2.** a **3.** a **4.** b **5.** b **6.** b **7.** a **8.** c **9.** a **10.** a
Skimming for Main Ideas: **1.** b **2.** c **3.** a **4.** b
Scanning for Details: **1.** T **2.** F **3.** T **4.** F **5.** F **6.** F **7.** T **8.** T **9.** T **10.** F
Order of Events: 6, 2, 5, 1, 7, 4, 3
Making Inferences and Drawing Conclusions: **1.** c **2.** c **3.** a

Unit 22
Vocabulary: **1.** b **2.** a **3.** b **4.** b **5.** a **6.** b **7.** a **8.** a **9.** a **10.** c
Skimming for Main Ideas: **1.** a **2.** c **3.** a **4.** b
Scanning for Details: **1.** Correct **2.** Correct **3.** Correct **4.** ~~the same~~/a different **5.** Correct **6.** ~~II~~/I; ~~USO~~/Salvation Army **7.** ~~Tennessee~~/Oklahoma **8.** ~~sugarcane~~/tree sap **9.** Correct **10.** ~~an unusual treat~~/a popular food; ~~east~~/west
Order of Events: 6, 2, 3, 1, 4, 5
Making Inferences and Drawing Conclusions: **1.** b **2.** b **3.** c

Unit 23
Vocabulary: **1.** contact sport **2.** opponent **3.** To ban **4.** extravaganza **5.** substituted **6.** squads **7.** Strategy **8.** banners **9.** Drills **10.** Floats
Skimming for Main Ideas: **1.** a **2.** b **3.** c **4.** c
Scanning for Details: **1.** c **2.** b **3.** b **4.** c **5.** a **6.** c **7.** b **8.** a **9.** c **10.** a
Order of Events: 2, 4, 6, 5, 3, 1
Making Inferences and Drawing Conclusions: **1.** b **2.** c **3.** a

Unit 24
Vocabulary: **1.** Rural **2.** Grief **3.** sentimental **4.** reflects **5.** Porches **6.** To mourn **7.** transitions **8.** lyrics **9.** environments **10.** incorporated
Skimming for Main Ideas: **1.** b **2.** a **3.** c **4.** a
Scanning for Details: **1.** ~~France and Spain~~/Scotland and Ireland **2.** Correct **3.** ~~urban~~/rural **4.** Correct **5.** ~~southwestern~~/southeastern; ~~the Rockies~~/Appalachia **6.** Correct **7.** Correct **8.** Correct **9.** ~~dreams and happiness~~/love and heartache **10.** ~~hasn't changed enough over the years~~/has gone too far from its original sound
Order of Events: 1, 4, 6, 2, 3, 5
Making Inferences and Drawing Conclusions: **1.** a **2.** c **3.** b